Braun

KT-165-501

Do Something Different

WITHDRAWN

Do Something Different

Proven Marketing Techniques to Transform Your Business

Jurgen Wolff

This edition first published in Great Britain in 2005 by
Virgin Books Ltd
Thames Wharf Studios
Rainville Road
London
W6 9HA

First published in 2001 by Virgin Publishing Ltd

Copyright © Jurgen Wolff 2001

The right of Jurgen Wolff to be identified as the Author of this Work has
been asserted by him in accordance with the Copyright, Designs and Patents
Act, 1988.

This book is sold subject to the condition that it shall not, by way of trade or
otherwise, be lent, resold, hired out or otherwise circulated without the
publisher's prior written consent in any form of binding or cover other than
that in which it is published and without a similar condition including this
condition being imposed on the subsequent purchaser.

A catalogue record for this book is available from the British Library.

ISBN 0 7535 0993 8

Series Consultant: Professor David Storey
Joint Series Editors: Robert Craven, Grier Palmer

Whilst care has been taken in the preparation of this book, no responsibility
for any loss occasioned to any person acting or refraining from any action as a
result of any material in this publication can be accepted by the author or
publisher or anyone connected with the series. Views expressed in this
publication are not necessarily those of Warwick Business School or the
University of Warwick.

Series design by Janice Mather at Ben Cracknell Studios
Typeset by Phoenix Photosetting, Chatham, Kent
Printed and bound in Italy

Dedicated to Sheridan
and the rest of the Brainstorm Marketing Team

Acknowledgements

Thanks to Craig Newman and Lizz Clarke for allowing their interviews to be used; to the editorial team at Virgin for daring to do something different; to all the marketers cited in this book; and to the advertising genius George Lois for giving inspiration to those who have a Big Idea.

Contents

Series Foreword
by Sir Richard Branson

I have always learnt my business on the job – from setting up *Student* magazine way back in 1967 right through to running the Virgin Group in the twenty-first century as one of the biggest brands in the world – rather than from a book, which makes it novel to be writing this foreword for the new editions of the Virgin Business Guide series.

I wouldn't call myself a marketing expert or a finance professional, however, nor am I the best person to do each and every job in the company – that's what I employ great staff for! And on a day-to-day basis, whatever the size of your company, you'll probably have advisers for all aspects of your business – from planning your next move to marketing and PR; from finance to problem solving and how to look after your customers – and these advisers are essential. At Virgin I do believe it is *my* job, though, to make the best possible decisions and that is only feasible if I know enough about each aspect of my business to make informed choices.

Learning from other people's business successes and failures can be an essential part of your own success. When I've experienced setbacks in my own business life, I have picked myself up again and had another go using the knowledge that I've gained from that failure. I have also always found advice from someone who's tried something similar before you – such as from Freddie Laker of Laker Airways when it came to running Virgin Atlantic and dealing with some of the early problems we encountered, or from Per

Lindstrand, who introduced me to ballooning and taught me much of what I know about it – one of the most important aspects of running my business. Even if, when it comes to it, I make my own decisions.

This series of books, in conjunction with Warwick Business School, is all written by businessmen and women who have been in business themselves and are therefore aware of the importance of information and the pitfalls you might come across. Not only that, but they include advice, ideas and case studies from many other successful and less successful businesspeople to help you.

The foundation upon which Virgin is built is doing things differently to other people or businesses in the same field – our stated objective is to 'shake things up' and we always try to do things in an innovative way. If Virgin sold socks, we'd probably sell them in packs of three as one always gets lost in the wash! I believe there is always a different way to go about things, whether in marketing your business externally as Jurgen Wolff discusses in *Do Something Different* or in running your business internally. This book shows you 'simple, inexpensive ways to make your product and service stand out in this crowded marketplace' – the same issue all companies face – and how doing something in a different way could help you and your business.

The figures speak for themselves – about half of small businesses fail in the first four years – so in whatever industry you work you need all the help you can get to succeed. And, above all, you should be having fun. Use these books as your tools, follow the advice and then make your own decisions – after all, you're the boss!

Preface

It is very difficult to stop the small-business owner talking about their enterprise – it is their passion, their livelihood and their hobby. Yet the listener or even the customer does not always share this enthusiasm. Even a University Professor of Enterprise may not share it!

But there are many occasions when I can feel the upsurge of the 'smile factor' during my conversations with small business owners. They describe what they do and how they go about it, and you find yourself thinking, 'Yes . . . that's really neat!' Nearly always this happens when somebody describes a very simple variation upon a common theme . . . so simple that nobody has done it before! Examples are selling to a totally different group of people or selling something slightly different from the competition. It is what economists call 'creating a niche' and it stems from doing something different. It is this that generates the smile factor.

Jurgen Wolff's book is about the smile factor. It is about doing something different. It is about placing the customer first, understanding that customer and then fully satisfying those needs.

When we at the SME Centre have looked at rapidly growing businesses, we constantly find that at the heart of their success is doing something different for the customer. That is why this book is so important.

But say you are already running a successful small business, perhaps even one based on having done something different for your customers in the past. Do you need to read this book? The answer is, undoubtedly, yes. Our research indicates that even good ideas, or doing something different, have only a short shelf life. The analogy we use is that of a surfboarder. If you run a small business, since we assume you can't control the waves, the skill is being on top of the board at the time at which the wave breaks. This rushes you forward and your business grows – provided you stay on the board!

But the wave peters out and you have to be ready to take advantage of the next wave. So, even if you have had a good idea, you need to be getting ready to do something different again to take advantage of the next wave. If you don't then you'll just drift.

Jurgen Wolff's book provides a variety of ideas taken from examples of those who have successfully ridden the waves. The book is based around fourteen principles. Each principle covers a key theme and there is a consistent structure in which several cases are provided to illustrate the theme. Most importantly there is a wide range of practical tips designed to stimulate the reader into asking themselves what this means for their business.

So, are you ready to ride the next wave?

Professor David Storey
Director, Centre for Small and Medium Sized Enterprises
Warwick Business School, University of Warwick

Introduction

 I hope you're feeling frustrated

I hope you're feeling frustrated because you have a great business or service, or idea for one, but you don't know how to make people aware of it without spending hundreds of thousands of pounds on advertising.

I hope you're feeling annoyed that your competitors are making a lot of money yet not providing as good a product or service as you can or do.

And I hope that you're ready to take charge of this situation and do something different.

If so, you've come to the right place. This book will show you how others have done something different in order to succeed, and how you can, too. You are about to learn simple, inexpensive ways to make your product or service stand out in this crowded marketplace.

You are about to learn the fourteen principles for marketing in this new world, and to read a hundred case studies that show you how to turn the principles into action.

What you will learn from the case studies

There is a saying that people can be divided into three groups: those who make things happen, those who watch things happen, and those who wonder what happened. Our case studies introduce you to people who made things happen. In each case, we'll look at six elements:

1. The problem
What was the goal?

2. The strategy
How did the people involved reach their goal?

3. The outcome
How well did their attempts work? Most of these are case studies in which the goals were attained. It's important to remember, however, that doing anything different means taking a risk. A particular approach may not work. When this happens, most people draw one of two negative conclusions:

> ■ This approach didn't work, so I'd better try the same thing again
> ■ This approach didn't work, so I'd better give up

That's why most people never get where they want to go. Consider how much better your chances are of being successful if you draw these two positive conclusions:

> ■ This approach didn't work, but I still believe in my goal
> ■ This approach didn't work, so I'd better try something different

There is a principle called 'requisite variety'. In simple terms, it says that the person who has at his or her disposal the greatest variety of means of reaching a goal is the person most likely to reach that goal. When you read the stories of people who have been the most successful, usually you will find they experienced many 'failures' before they attained their success; for most overnight wonders, it was a long night.

4. The lessons
What each case study can teach us about breakthrough marketing.

5. Questions to ask yourself

Questions that help you relate the methods in the case studies to your own situation.

6. Tips

And tips to do likewise.

The idea is not that you copy the case studies exactly, but that you use your own creativity to adapt them to your situation. After all, everything that appears to be new is, in fact, a mixture of what already exists. For example, McDonald's was not a totally new idea. It combined two older ideas: a snack bar and the assembly line. Similarly, the successful new book chains, such as Borders, have combined book buying with library lounging and come up with settings in which you can sit in a comfy chair and read before you buy.

I don't know which two or three approaches in this book you will combine or adapt in order to come up with a new strategy that catapults your business ahead of your competitors – I only know that the opportunity is here, waiting for you.

Going from ideas to action

The first step is to read through the book with pen and paper handy so you can jot down your ideas for how you, too, can do something different to help people find out about why they should be doing business with you. Often, I suggest that you brainstorm ideas. Brainstorming is more than just sitting around trying to think of ideas: there are specific techniques you can use to generate an endless flow of ideas. To help you do that, I've included a chapter on brainstorming techniques you can put into use immediately.

The next step is to devise a marketing plan based on the new ideas you want to implement. The final section shows you how to move from the idea stage to action, then to evaluation, and on to keeping the process going, so that you are constantly finding new ways of keeping your business in the public's mind. This section includes interviews with two top marketing professionals, who share with you the secret of how they work with both large and small companies to create successful brands.

Even after you've worked through the book and put your new marketing plan into action, we will offer you further support at the BrainstormNet.com website. There, you will find (free) constantly updated additional case studies and tips for keeping up with the ever-changing marketplace. In fact, when you've used the principles in this book to reach new heights of success and profit, I hope you'll let us know, so that we can feature your company as a case study that can inspire others to succeed, too. Let's get started!

It's about what *they* want, not about what *you* want

Customers have an ever-increasing supply of people and companies willing to give them exactly what they want. Yet many companies still act as though we were in the days when Henry Ford said, 'You can have any colour, as long as it's black.' To be effective, you must know exactly what your potential customers want.

The following case studies will show you how successful business people learn from prospective customers, current customers, and even ex-customers.

Plant the seeds of success

The problem

OM Scott, a retailer of seeds, lawn-care products and the like, wanted to sell more goods. However, their products, while good, were no better than those of their competitors, so they needed to do something to differentiate themselves.

The strategy

They went to their customers and found out what problems they had with lawn care. The complaint that came up again and again was how difficult people found it to plant their lawn in a controlled way, rather than putting too many seeds in one spot and not enough in another. Scott decided to concentrate on how they could help solve this problem. They came up with the Scott Spreader, a small wheelbarrow that has holes in it and can be adjusted to control the flow of seeds.

The outcome

The Scott Spreader itself made millions, and the company became the market leader in its field.

The lessons

The company started by looking at what they needed (a bigger share of the market), but then shifted their view to that of the customer. By asking what the customers needed, they were able to solve the customers' problems and their own. They also looked beyond their normal activities. By enlarging the scope of their activities they were able to make a big difference to the core of their business.

Questions to ask yourself

1 Have you fully considered what your potential customers need? What are the problems they have in relation to your area of business?
2 How can you help them solve this problem?
3 Is there any way that going beyond your normal activities will help you to achieve your goals?

Tips: Win customers by solving their problems

1 Begin by being aware of your customers' problems. The easiest way is to ask the people concerned: what really annoys them, or which one thing would make their life easier?
2 Focus all your attention on how the problem can be solved. Don't worry initially how this relates to your business. Brainstorm lots of possible solutions before starting to judge which ones might be best.

3 When you have come up with some promising solutions, consider how these can relate to your business. It may be simply that you offer the idea of the solution to customers, which will win you goodwill. Or it may be that the solution gives you an idea for a new product that you will manufacture yourself, or produce in collaboration with another company.

Train them to buy

The problem

The author Tanya Sassoon wanted to show publishers that there would be a market for her unusual product, the Boyfriend Training Kit. It comes in a brown envelope and contains a small book of rules, another book for noting the boyfriend's offences, yellow stickers to use as warning cards, and so forth.

The strategy

Sassoon made the training kit part of her arts degree course and made seventy copies to offer for sale at London's ICA Bookshop (known to handle avant-garde products).

The outcome

The ICA Bookshop accepted the copies, and they sold out within a few weeks. This so impressed Bloomsbury Publishing (publishers of the Harry Potter books) that they bought the world rights to the product, and are considering coming out with a whole series of similar humorous training kits.

The lessons

If you can show some previous level of acceptance for your product or service, you are more likely to be accepted further down the line. Furthermore, getting feedback from a limited trial can be useful. In this case, the product received a good reception, but, had that not been the case, the author could have tried varying the product or the packaging or the price or another element to see whether that increased the customer response.

Questions to ask yourself

1   If your target customers are likely to be sceptical, where else can you offer your product or service first where it is more likely to be accepted?
2   How can you document the initial success of your product or service in a way that will impress the next buyer?
3   How can you use a trial run like this to gather useful feedback and, if necessary, adjust your product or service?

Tips: How to get a positive test group

1   Start with people who are likely to be most interested in your product or service. In our case study, the author didn't approach a suburban bookshop: she went to one that appeals to a young and arty crowd. These were the types of trendsetter customers who typically love anything new and different.
2   Consider giving away samples of your product or letting people sample your service, and then getting feedback from them. Or at least start with a price that is appealing and lowers the barriers to buying. (However, at times a low price may not be appropriate – trendy buyers are suspicious that low-cost items are not exclusive enough.)
3   Consider piggybacking on to a product or service that people already like. For example, some online booksellers are offering a free download of the first chapter of a new mystery book to customers who order a similar book.

The more the better

The problem

Ford wanted to make sure that their Windstar minivan would appeal to all kinds of customer.

The strategy

Ford put a number of women on the design team of the Windstar. This is one of a number of strategies Ford use to make sure they get the widest possible spectrum of input when designing automobiles. Other strategies include hiring people from a variety of backgrounds, and having a Take Our Daughters to Work Day during which they ask kids to react to their cars. They also have a lease programme for employees, during which they ask the employees' spouses for their reactions to various features of the cars.

The outcome

A number of design features for the successful Windstar were added as a result of the diversity of input. One example: the overhead light's 'sleeping-baby mode'. This makes it possible to have only the floor lighting turn on when a door is opened, because the illumination of the overhead light might wake a sleeping child.

The lessons

If your product or service is going to be used by a variety of people, it makes sense to ask those kinds of people for their input during the design or development stage, or when considering how to upgrade what you already offer. It's important not to miss the valuable information that can come from those not normally asked (e.g., children).

Questions to ask yourself

1 Have you allowed all the types of potential users of your product or service to have input?
2 If not, how can you reach them and motivate them to give you the benefit of their ideas?

Tips: How to get customer input

1 After customers have had long enough to use the product, send them a brief questionnaire via post or email. To motivate them to answer, offer either a small payment or a discount on another product you sell, or have a prize draw among all the respondents.
2 Invite a small group of customers to a pizza dinner, and guide a discussion about what they like or don't like about your product or service, and how they think it could be improved.

If you have the discussion led by someone who is not part of your company, the customers may be more frank and forthcoming.

3 Make sure that whoever at your company deals with complaints keeps a written record of them. Review these periodically to see whether they offer clues about how you can improve your business.

Stannard's theory of customer wants

The problem

The physics professor Russell Stannard wanted to write (and find a publisher for) a book that would entertainingly help youngsters learn about physics, especially Einstein's Theory of Relativity.

The strategy

To find out what his ultimate customers (children) liked, Stannard spent many hours in his local library, looking through children's books and counting up the date stamps to see how often books had been borrowed. He analysed the most popular books to see what they had in common. His findings: illustrations, lots of dialogue, humour, short chapters and characters the readers could identify with.

Next he needed to know how much children might already know about the subject, so he did a survey of 250 twelve-year-olds to assess their awareness of topics such as gravity and acceleration.

Using this information, he wrote the book *Black Holes and Uncle Albert*, and was able to show publishers that it was based on solid information about the target audience.

The outcome

Even with all of his preparation, Stannard had to send his manuscript to eighteen publishers before it was accepted by Faber & Faber. Since then, the book and a companion volume called *The Time and Space of Uncle Albert* have become popular sellers.

The lessons

Stannard knew that, if he'd *asked* young readers their criteria for an enjoyable book, they might not have been able to articulate them. Instead, he was creative about getting information from his target group indirectly – via their behaviour. In assessing the needs and wants of your target customer, finding ways of measuring their actual behaviour can lead to more accurate results than simply asking them – a fact that poll takers have known for a long time.

To check the end users' knowledge, Stannard employed the more straightforward method of a survey – another tool you may find useful.

Stannard combined the results to create a product that is satisfying at the educational level and the entertainment level – both of which were also strong selling points when he was marketing the book to publishers. Furthermore, it gave the publishers the option of using this as a selling point to the book buyers (who would usually be parents, not the children themselves). In other words, your research can itself become a sales and marketing tool.

Questions to ask yourself

1 Do you really know what your customers want? Can you summarise it in a few key points?
2 If you're going only by what customers say, how can you check whether their behaviour verifies this?
3 Is there a way that you can use your research into customers' wants and needs as a marketing point in itself, to show them how in tune you are with them?

Tips: Finding out all you can about your customers

1 First, decide what it is you really need and want to know about your customers. Don't worry at this stage how you will get the information.
2 Next, consider where you can find a lot of your customers in one place, if possible. Example: if you're selling to people interested in consumer electronics, consider the large trade fairs that draw such people in several major cities.

3　Now brainstorm all the possible ways you might get the desired information. These include questionnaires, opinion polls, focus groups and observation (at a trade fair, for instance, notice which booths have most visitors; at your booth or that of a competitor selling similar goods, listen for what questions visitors ask most often). Certain types of statistical information, of course, are available from local or national government offices and business organisations, including chambers of commerce.

Follow the trend

The problem

The Koala Corporation wanted to broaden its business from its initial offering: fold-out, plastic nappy-changing stations for toilets in stores, restaurants and petrol stations.

The strategy

The company recognised that the increase in single-parent families and dual-career families means that a lot of adults can't go anywhere without taking their children along. This suggested a great opportunity for selling products that make public places more children-friendly. The company decided to supply indoor and outdoor play equipment, children's furniture, play tunnels and other things that divert children while their parents are shopping. The appeal to businesses is obvious: it's difficult for a salesperson to keep a parent's attention if an unhappy child is tugging at Mummy's or Daddy's hands, wanting to go home.

The outcome

In a recent five-year period, sales more than tripled, and, in the last year of that period, profits rose by 25 per cent. The company also reports interest from supermarket chains that are considering building separate play areas for children.

The lessons

It's risky being a one-product company, and generally the best way to branch out is to find new products or services that relate in some way to what you are doing successfully already. While predicting trends can be risky, there are certain demographic developments, such as the increase in single-parent families, that are a safe basis for expanding a business.

Questions to ask yourself

1. Are you danger of relying too much on one product or type of service?
2. Is there a social trend that suggests a new direction for your business?

Tips: Following the trends

1. Long-term forecasts are risky, but shorter-term trends are easier to spot. Read widely to be aware of the direction in which things are going. Don't read only those publications that target your age group, but keep an eye on what is being talked about in magazines for youngsters and oldsters as well.
2. At least once per quarter, take the time to get together with colleagues to summarise your observations and theirs about the social trends that seem to be emerging. A colleague may spot something that you would have missed.
3. Consider how all of these trends, not just the ones with obvious relevance to your business, might impact upon what you do, or what your customers may want from you in the future. Also, consider the knock-on effects of trends, and how those second-step changes might affect you.

Room for improvement

The problem

After a long period of relatively successful performance, Boston Acoustics, maker of stereo speakers, ran into a period of fewer sales and wild swings in earnings. The challenge was to boost sales to previous levels and beyond.

The strategy

The normal strategy might have been to get more retail outlets. However, that would have hurt the company's relationship with loyal distributors and increased overhead. Instead, the company decided to take a close look at their products and realised that their line needed improvement. They upped their research and development from 4 per cent of annual sales to over 6 per cent.

The outcome

The firm developed a new range of indoor/outdoor speakers and made deals with computer manufacturers to supply high-quality PC speakers. Revenues rose more than 60 per cent.

The lessons

When earnings decline, it's easy to blame retailers or to assume that the focus should be on finding ways to sell more of the same product or service. However, it can be worthwhile to take a critical look at what is being offered. The way out of the problem may be a needed boost to the quality of existing products or the development of new ones.

Questions to ask yourself

1 Are there aspects of your product or service that may be outdated or ripe for improvement?
2 Could you gain significant benefits by upping your investment in research and development that could lead to new or improved products or services?

Tips: Taking another look

1 Ask an outsider (not a competitor, of course) to take a totally fresh look at your business and report back his or her impressions of all aspects of it. A consultant will charge a lot of money for this, while someone working directly for you may be too close to the issue to have a fresh perspective;

therefore it may be wise to consult an acquaintance who is in a different line of business and brings an objective view to the process.

2 Brainstorm how an increase in your research and development could pay off and determine where these resources would be most productive. Although research and development in large companies can cost millions, this idea applies to small companies, too, and even to individuals. In these cases, the research may be as simple as conducting a survey of customers, or hiring a student to observe customer behaviour for a fewdays.

Who isn't being served?

The problem

Sony's PlayStation wanted to be on a par with Nintendo and Sega in the games business.

The strategy

Believing that the two main competitors had focused too much on one slice of the consumers – namely, boys from ten to sixteen years old – PlayStation decided to put considerable resources into wooing potential customers who had never played, or had stopped when they got older.

The outcome

Sony has had good results with a number of offbeat games. One was called Parappa the Rapper, which sold over 700,000 copies in Japan alone, and appealed mostly to players in their twenties. The games market is still hotly contested, but the PlayStation's wider range of games has helped it to stay competitive.

The lessons

If you are in a business in which everyone is competing for the same group of customers, it can be worth asking whether there are potential customers who are being ignored. While it may require additional effort to bring your product or service to the attention of these people, being the first to serve them may make them enthusiastic converts to your business.

Questions to ask yourself

1 Is there a group of people being ignored by your business?
2 Is there a way you could appeal to them?
3 What would be the economic impact if you were successful?

Tips: Finding underserved customers

1 Identify the kinds of customers you are currently serving, and the types who are not your customers (a variety of criteria can apply here, including age, level of affluence, geographic location, ethnic background, sexual preference – just about any way that we can categorise people).
2 For each of the groups not being served by your business, is it also true that they tend to be ignored by your competitors?
3 For each of the groups not being served by your type of business, brainstorm how you could modify or adapt your business or service to appeal to this untapped group. Even if you find only one match, you may have discovered a great new source of revenue.

Your marketing techniques must be congruent with your product or service

First impressions are incredibly important, and people will judge you and your product or service by your marketing. For example, if the key attribute of what you are offering is integrity, your marketing efforts must suggest strong integrity; if you are offering a fun product or service, the marketing itself should be fun and entertaining.

Generally, the nature of the product or service sets the tone, but sometimes the tone itself becomes dominant. An example of this is the Virgin brand, which started with publications and music (perfect for fun and entertaining marketing) and has become so strong that Richard Branson is trying to apply the same tone to products and services (such as financial advice) that are normally seen as sober and conservative.

The congruence should extend to your image as well (see Principle 7). When your product, your image and your marketing efforts are all aligned, they add up to a very powerful force.

A (very) personal approach

The problem

How to be considered for employment when no one is interviewing. In this case, the job seekers were Paul Gaye (24 at the time) and Steve Reeves (22 at the time), who were hoping to secure jobs, or at least an internship, at a major London advertising agency. This was at a time when a slowing economy had wreaked havoc in the advertising world, and there were few, if any, new positions open.

The strategy

Gaye and Reeves wrote an identical letter to every creative director in London (who were all men). In each case, the director received a letter written on pink, perfumed paper. The letter started: 'Dear [name of director], You probably won't remember my name ... ' and alluded to a passionate evening in a car park 23 years before. The outcome of that night was twins: Steve and Paul. The letter finished with the statement, 'They're trying to get into advertising and I hear you're quite good at that sort of thing.' Enclosed was a Polaroid photo of the young men.

The outcome

Only one director failed to respond, the others were appreciative and several wanted to meet the young applicants. One of the directors, Tony Cox, gave them a job and kept the letter on display in his office for a long time afterwards.

The lessons

Gaye and Reeves used an unusual manner of demonstrating their creativity (a fictional personal letter rather than a résumé or typical letter asking for a job), and they used an unusual delivery mode (a pink perfumed envelope addressed in handwriting in green ink, marked 'personal'). Since their creativity was what they were trying to sell, this marketing approach was perfect.

Questions to ask yourself

1   Is there an unusual manner of packaging your letter or proposal that might draw attention to it? Is it appropriate to the idea or project you are trying to sell?
2   How can you arouse the curiosity of your target audience in a way that fits with the nature of your product or service?

3   How can you use a manner of approaching your target that shows how qualified you are to benefit them in some way?

Tips: How to open closed doors

1   Consider how to get yourself, or your message, past the usual gatekeepers. For example, most secretaries would not open a letter with a handwritten address and marked 'personal', and the young applicants in our case study were able to take advantage of that. However, had they merely been sending a conventional CV and used that trick, it probably would have annoyed the recipients. In this case, the amusement value of the contents of the letter made up for the transgression. Therefore, be sure that, if you use a technique like that, the recipients will find the message entertaining.

2   Keep in mind the nature of the person you are trying to reach. The technique above probably would not have worked as well in the world of banking, but was perfect for the field of advertising, in which playfulness performs an important role.

3   Consider how you can apply your strategy to several people, so that, if one or several don't respond, you'll still have a chance. In this case, the young men sent an identical letter to a number of people, and they needed to succeed with only one in order to achieve their objective. They also sent all the letters out at once, rather than one after the other – whenever possible, simultaneous submissions are best.

Short cut to success

The problem

The promoter of a New York animated-film festival wanted to broaden its appeal.

The strategy

The promoter, Terry Thoren, bought a thousand pairs of boxer shorts from a wholesaler, got together a bunch of friends and colleagues, provided them with rock music, beer and pizza, and had them stamp cartoon images on to the underwear. The boxer shorts were sent to New York's movers and shakers, along with the note, 'These aren't just animated shorts'.

The outcome

The event garnered huge amounts of publicity, and sold out.

The lessons

The promoter found a perfect match between his event and his 'do something different' way of promoting it. Sending underwear with cartoons on it was irreverent, fun and funky – just like the film festival it was promoting. Naturally, it would not have been appropriate for something like the opening of a medical clinic; the lesson is to find a marketing technique that reflects the nature of the product itself.

Questions to ask yourself

1. What adjectives would you use to describe your product or service?
2. What adjectives would you use to describe your current marketing efforts?
3. If the two don't match, what changes can you make?
4. What additional marketing efforts can you think of that match the nature of your business? (If you're not sure, find the case studies for the businesses that most closely match your own and use them for inspiration.)

Tips: More ways to do something different

1. Create, or have an artist create, a cartoon character that matches your business and use it to attract attention (this could include using it in ads, having a costume maker create a costume of the character that an actor can wear at your business or at a trade show, or featuring a comic strip with this character in it in your newsletter).
2. Publish a book of cartoons that relate to your type of business and give copies to potential customers.

3 Get a troupe of local actors to do comedy sketches in your store to celebrate an anniversary or special sale, and invite the public.

Find your fans

The problem

When Mel and Howard Lev opened a Krispy Kreme doughnut outlet in New York City, few people there were familiar with the product, which had a big following in the South. How to spread the word?

The strategy

In addition to a traditional public relations campaign, the father-and-son team conducted a direct-mail campaign inviting the alumni of Southern universities living in New York to an opening party.

The outcome

The party was a roaring success, and so was the outlet. The Levs were given franchising rights for New York and New Jersey, and have expanded to nine outlets.

The lessons

When introducing a product or service, it pays to find people who are already fans. They may not constitute the bulk of your customers, but they are the ones who will pass along enthusiastic word-of-mouth reports. Even if they are scattered, there is usually a way to find them.

Questions to ask yourself

1 If you are starting a new business, what kinds of people are most likely to be fans? In our example, most of the alumni had probably encountered Krispy Kreme doughnuts in their childhood. The same strategy could work if you are merely

offering the same type of product or service with which people might already be familiar in another context.

2 How can you reach these people?

3 What would get to these people to try your product or service? (In our example, a party was the draw.)

Tips: Finding fans

1 Do a brainstorming session in which you come up with as many words as possible to describe the kinds of people likely to enjoy what you are offering. These words might describe types of people (for instance, students, older people, pet owners), or qualities that such people might have (home-loving, say, or excitement-craving or status-conscious).

2 For each of the types of people, brainstorm where or how you are likely to find them. What kind of websites would they visit? What kinds of public events would they attend? What kinds of publications do they read? What kinds of catalogues do they use when shopping?

3 When you've finished the second step, see which of these avenues are most practical for you to use to connect with these potential customers.

4 Decide what would give these people an incentive to try your product or service. This might be a public event if you're trying to reach people within a small geographical area, or a discount offer, or a membership scheme with special benefits.

Sell your message

The problem

The monks in a Benedictine Abbey needed to find a way to support their monastery.

The strategy

They offered a series of business ethics courses aimed at industry leaders.

The outcome

The courses, which run for three to five days and cost between £325 and £1,250, have been a huge success. Among those taking part have been managers of the hotel group Novotel, which has adapted aspects of the rules of St Benedict on hospitality. The monks could run many more courses, but are keen to make sure that this valuable sideline does not detract from their main vocation.

The lessons

In this case, the product was a direct outcome of who the monks are and what they represent. It may be that your business has within it some spin-off possibilities that could add valuable revenue and still be congruent with your main mission. Examples: a restaurant could offer cooking classes; a vet's practice could offer presentations on animal care; an accounting practice could offer workshops on keeping good financial records.

Questions to ask yourself

1. Are there aspects of your business that represent value that you could offer in order to bring in additional revenue?
2. Are these opportunities congruent with your larger mission?

Tips: Selling more of what you have to offer

1. Make a list of all the knowledge and skills that are represented in your company.
2. Brainstorm how each of these could be spun off into a subsidiary product or service.
3. For the most promising ones, consider whether and how they might add to the value of your primary product or service. For example, cooking classes held at a restaurant could garner publicity, and bring in new customers from among the students.

Be on their side

The problem

Amilya Antonetti wanted to break into the American laundry-detergent market, which is dominated by brand giants such as Tide and Clorox.

The strategy

Antonetti decided to fill a niche in the market with hypoallergenic cleaning products, and to establish a close relationship with her customers. She represented SoapWorks as a company established by a mother for mothers (her own young son had suffered reactions to the chemicals in traditional washing powders).

To make her customers her best salespeople, Antonetti establishes a close bond with them. She personally takes many of the hundred or so phone calls a day the company receives from customers; she appears on local radio and television stations to give advice; she is the voice of her own radio adverts; and she gives away more than a hundred thousand free samples to children's hospitals and women's shelters.

The outcome

Antonetti's products are now on sale in more than 2,500 stores across America, and in 1999 her sales revenues were $5 million. When one supermarket chain took SoapWorks products off their shelves, a customer rebellion forced them to restore them.

The lessons

Even in a market dominated by giant companies and well-known brands, there are niches to be found and exploited. Also, customers are the best allies in persuading stores to carry a product. The best way to win over customers is to be their ally and show a personal interest in their problems and welfare.

Questions to ask yourself

1   Is there a market niche you are overlooking because you have felt that the field is too dominated by bigger players?

2 Have you established a close enough relationship with your customers?
3 If not, what means could you use to get closer to them?
4 Are there ways your most loyal customers could help you get the word out about your product or service?

Tips: Getting customers to work for you

1 Communicate regularly with your best customers. Depending on the nature of your business, this might involve ringing them, publishing a newsletter, sponsoring events to which they are invited and appearing on radio and television.
2 Show a genuine interest in solving their problems. Make sure that your customers have a way of registering complaints, and handle them quickly and with generosity. The saying is that one satisfied customer will tell ten people how good your business is; one *dis*satisfied customer will tell a *hundred* people how *bad* your business is. Whenever possible, convert an unhappy customer into a happy one.
3 Show that you are contributing to the community. This may include making a financial donation to a charity of your choice, but getting involved more directly is a better way of becoming known. Donations of materials or goods (as in our example) may win you more converts to your business than simply handing over cash.

Start with the right people

The problem

Mickey Shulhof, vice-chairman of Sony USA in the 1970s, wanted to sell the idea of CDs to industry executives. However, they were more intent on protecting their investment in LP vinyl records.

The strategy

Schulhof thought about who would be interested in a medium that was capable of better sound quality. He realised that the prime group was the recording artists themselves. He approached them and demonstrated the capabilities of CD technology.

The outcome

When top recording artists became enthusiastic about CDs, music industry executives became willing to take another look at the technology as well. Ironically, the entire industry eventually made billions of pounds because most music fans bought CD versions of the music collections they already owned on vinyl.

The lessons

This is a good example of picking a marketing strategy that is congruent with the product – the people who would care most about sound quality would be the musicians. Therefore, they offered a way into the marketplace, even though success also required the co-operation of many other elements of the music industry. Starting with the people most likely to be enthusiastic about your business is usually a good way to gain some precious momentum at the beginning of a new enterprise.

Questions to ask yourself

1 If you are trying to win converts to your business or new idea, who are the people who would be most likely to be enthusiastic about it?
2 How can you most easily get to these people?
3 How can you demonstrate to these people the appeal of your business or idea?
4 How can you encourage the first converts to spread the word?

Tips: Winning over the first converts

1 When you have identified who are the people likely to be most enthusiastic about your product or service, brainstorm the best way to get them to try it. It can be worthwhile to offer them free samples, or the loan of a more expensive product, or a free service.
2 Get the first-users to give you unpaid testimonials for your

product or service. If appropriate, see if you can get a picture of them using your product, and permission to include it in your sales literature or publicity materials. This is especially useful if the person is a celebrity.

3 Also, brainstorm whether there are any groups of customers you are missing out, whose conversion might give you publicity even if it's not a big enough group to target for purely financial reasons. For example, the owner of a grocery delivery service might offer to make free deliveries to hospitals or old people's homes, which would make an excellent human-interest story for the local and national press and lead to positive publicity.

Ask and you shall receive (probably)

Asking for what you want is one of the simplest and easiest marketing techniques, and yet the most neglected. This isn't just about asking for the sale in your sales material or presentations: it's also about asking for help, support, advice and endorsements. Your mother was right: 'The worst thing that could happen is that they'll say no.'

The early bird

The problem

How to bypass all the usual barriers to getting material to someone in a high position and get him to consider an idea for a movie. The target was Jeffrey Katzenberg, at that time one of Hollywood's busiest and most high-powered executives at Disney Studios.

The strategy

The writer David Peterson was aware that Katzenberg always arrived at the Disney studio notoriously early. Peterson got there even earlier. At four in the morning, he asked the security guard at the gate to pass along a package to Katzenberg when he arrived. Had the package been in the shape of a script, the guard probably would have declined (they've all been warned not to accept scripts, because most companies will not consider material that is not submitted by an agent). However, this was a small package and it wasn't ticking, so the guard took it.

When Katzenberg arrived, he opened the package and found an audio tape and a note that read, 'If you can spare 47 seconds, you might be interested in this tape.' That's about how long it took to drive from the gate to his parking spot, so he listened. On the audiocassette was a professionally produced radio promo for *Flyers*, a movie about female pilots in World War Two. There were snippets of dialogue, realistic dogfight sound effects and voice-over narration, even theme music, just as if the film had already been produced.

The outcome

Three days later, Peterson got a note from Katzenberg – yes, he would like to take a look at the script.

The lessons

Peterson did something different in two ways: he used a different medium (audio tape) from the one execs are used to (scripts or outlines); and he used a different delivery system. These got him through the usual barriers put up to keep out unsolicited material. Also, they were evidence of his creativity in what after all is a creative field. To do this, he first studied his target and used what he found out (that Katzenberg got to the studio very early) to help formulate his strategy.

He also took account of the fact that such people are very busy and let Katzenberg know that he knew it: by specifying that it would take only 47 seconds to listen to the tape, he increased the odds that the tape would be played.

Finally, he also took advantage of one of man's strongest drives: curiosity.

Questions to ask yourself

1 Is there an unusual but appropriate medium that you can employ in order to promote your own project?

2 Have you studied your target audience enough to come up with a different and appropriate way to approach them?

3 How are you letting your target audience know that what you want from them is consistent with their needs or limitations?

Tips: Getting past the barriers

1 Define what the barriers are to entry or to moving to a higher level of success in your field. In some cases, as in our example, it may be access to the decision makers. In others, it may be the requirement for expensive equipment. In yet others, it may be the difficulty of reaching a large customer base.

2 For each barrier, spend some time brainstorming ways around them. If you can't get to the decision makers at their offices, where else may they be found? On the golf course? At events benefiting their favourite charities? At their gym? If you can't afford the expensive equipment, is there a way to lease it? Or can you use someone else's during the hours they're not using it (say midnight to 6 a.m.)? If you can't afford advertising to make large numbers of potential customers aware of your company, can you use a zany publicity stunt to get coverage (you'll find several successful examples in this book)?

3 Keep your eyes open for accounts of how people in other lines of business got past barriers and brainstorm how you might adapt their strategies to yourself. For example, if you have not been able to get in to see a buyer for a major company, might it make sense to send him or her an audio cassette featuring brief testimonials from three of your satisfied customers, and then ask for a meeting at the end of the tape?

A job for Jobs

The problem

Twelve-year-old Steve Jobs wanted to find a summer job.

The strategy

He looked in the telephone book for the number of the billion-dollar firm Hewlett-Packard, asked to speak to its co-founder, Bill Hewlett, and asked for help.

The outcome

Hewlett initially gave Jobs parts for building his own electronic devices, and then gave him employment for the summer. At twelve, Steve Jobs had made his first power call. He went on to establish Apple computers, and years later returned to the company to rescue it from the brink of failure.

The lessons

Maybe it was his youthful naïveté that gave Jobs the brazenness to talk to the president of the company, or maybe it was his passion and determination to get involved with electronics. Either way, his example is one that we can learn from. The lesson is not only to ask, but to ask the right person. Go as high up the chain of command as you can. That's where the people are who can make decisions. Since they are successful themselves, they are more likely to admire (and respond to) your passion for your product or service.

Questions to ask yourself

1 What do you need in order to promote or market your business? Endorsements? Advice? Collaboration?
2 Who could give you what you need?
3 How can you reach them?
4 What's stopping you from contacting them to ask for what you need?

Tips: How to ask for what you need

1 If you have trouble getting up the nerve to ask someone high up for help, just remember that 'mother's statement': the worst that they can do is say no. As long as you accept a turn-down with good grace, people do not mind being asked for help. In fact, most of them had help in getting to the top

themselves, and consider it a moral obligation to help others on their way up, too.

2 Be very precise in stating what you need. 'I need help figuring out how to sell my product' is too general. 'I need help in figuring out how to reach retired naval officers' is specific. When you are clear about exactly what it is you need, the person you are asking can quickly determine whether or not they will be able to help you. If they are not, it is also easy for them to refer you to someone who could. That leads us to the next point …

3 If the person you are asking turns you down, always enquire whether they can refer you to someone who could help. Quite often this person turns out to be a better choice than the one you approached originally.

Don't wait for opportunity to knock

The problem

A small optical-effects company, Available Light Ltd, came across the script for the film *Ghost* before it was made and decided they wanted to work on the project even though they were unknown.

The strategy

Totally unsolicited, they did preliminary artwork showing how their effects would look, arranged to meet the producer and director, and presented their ideas.

The outcome

One of the Available Light partners, Van Vliet, told *Premiere* magazine, 'They were looking at us like, who are these crazy people? I have to admit, it was an unusual approach.' Nonetheless, they were hired.

The lessons

This is a great example of actively seeking opportunities rather than sitting back and waiting to be approached. Furthermore, it's another example of how it can pay off when we put in some effort without any guarantee of success. That almost always impresses the people with whom we hope to do business.

Questions to ask yourself

1 If you were to be more aggressive about seeking opportunities for your company, who could you approach?
2 What could you do, unasked, that would impress potential customers?

Tips: Finding opportunities

1 Make a list of people or companies who could possibly use your services but with whom you are not currently doing business.
2 For each one, brainstorm what would impress them. For example, might a sample of your product or service be individualised to their particular requirements?
3 For each one, brainstorm the best way to contact them or to get them to see the sample. Let yourself go, don't stick to just the usual methods. For example, if there is a hoarding near their company, might it be worth renting it and putting up a poster that relates their product to yours? Or at lunchtime, could you have some food delivered to them, along with a 'menu' of your products or services?

Do it your way

The problem

After World War Two, ten American ex-Army Air Force officers wanted to continue to work together, and to apply in business the statistical skills they had learned in wartime.

The strategy

They sent a telegram to the Ford Motor Company, offering their services as a group.

The outcome

Henry Ford II, who had just taken over the company, hired them. John A Bryne, author of the book *The Whizz Kids*, writes, 'As a group, they would become the very model of the modern professional manager.' They straightened out the finances of Ford and set the pattern for American industry as a whole.

The lessons

Despite the fact that employers were not used to hiring ten people in a group, the whizz kids decided to offer their services collectively. In other words, they weren't limited by how things were done: they suggested a new way of doing them.

They also decided to aim for the top, and made their proposal to one of the country's biggest firms.

Questions to ask yourself

1 Are you unquestioningly accepting that things relating to your business are done a certain way?
2 Can you think of new ways for things to be done, ones that might be unconventional but effective?
3 Who could you approach with these new ideas?

Tips: Doing things your way

1 Forget about how things are normally done, and make your starting point the way you would like to do them.
2 List all of the advantages of your way to the person or people you need to convince. In our example, Ford would be getting a strong team that worked well together previously and that had an impressive track record.
3 Whenever possible, go right to the top. The people lower down in the hierarchy tend to want to protect their positions, and may see any change in the status quo as a threat. It's usually the people at the top who are most open to bold new ideas.

Make them pay!

The problem

The Media Arts Group, a collection of 140 art galleries around America, wanted to find a way to avoid having to do expensive marketing.

The strategy

The group sells reproductions of the sentimental (and hugely popular) paintings of Thomas Kinkade. It established a collectors' club, which issues a quarterly newsletter with the latest news of his paintings. The twist: members have to pay $45 each to join the club.

The outcome

Over 11,000 people have joined the club and have helped spread the word. In a one-hour session on the home shopping channel QVC, Kinkade sold over $2 million worth of products. Furthermore, Media Arts has licensed Kinkade images to Hallmark, Avon and Crown Crafts, among others.

The lessons

When people become collectors or fans, they undergo a marvellous transformation. Suddenly they are willing to pay for the feeling of belonging to an exclusive group.

Questions to ask yourself

1 Is there any aspect of your business that lends itself to appealing to collectors or fans?
2 If so, how can you best capture their loyalty? This might mean forming a club, having an annual (or more frequent) live event for them, or creating a members-only website.
3 Can you get people to pay to belong and at the same time use them to spread word of mouth about your business?

Tips: Getting people to pay to belong

1 Give people the trappings of belonging: membership cards, badges, newsletters that go only to members, a website chat line that is open only to them, and so on. People love feeling that they belong to a group.

2 Create an aura of exclusivity around at least one aspect of your product line or your service. For example, certain products could be offered only to people who have joined the inner circle (for a fee), or who spend over a certain amount per year with you (the concept of the frequent-fliers club). If there is anything people love even more than belonging to a group, it's belonging to an exclusive group.

How to listen

The problem

Julian Metcalfe, co-founder of the Prêt à Manger coffee-and-sandwich shop chain, wanted to be sure that customers would have a quick and effective way to give the company feedback.

The strategy

He printed his name, company address and phone number on every Prêt bag and invited customers to ring him if they have a problem or a comment. He told *The Times*, 'I speak to every customer that calls … if someone has a problem with a £2 sandwich I write back to them the same day.' To extend this to improving communication with the Prêt employees, he also gave all of them his home telephone number.

The outcome

Prêt à Manger has been an enormous success, and set new standards in fast food. While Metcalfe's open-communication policy is undoubtedly not the only reason, it probably has contributed considerably.

The lessons

Interactivity is the order of the day, and most customers expect to find at least an e-mail address and ideally a freephone number to ring if they have a problem or a query. The easier you make it for people to let you know what they want, the easier you make it for yourself to meet their expectations and keep them as customers.

Questions to ask yourself

1 Do you make it easy for customers to contact you?
2 Do you make it easy for employees to contact you?
3 What methods come to mind that you could use to improve your communication with both groups?
4 In the past thirty days, what have you learned from your customers that has led you to change some aspect of what you do? If there's nothing, maybe you're not asking them persuasively enough.

Tips: Listening to your customers

1 Make it easy for customers to find you. Print a phone number, address, and/or website address on all of your materials and invite comments and complaints.
2 Be prompt in responding to enquiries or complaints. The longer unhappy customers have to wait for an answer, the unhappier they get.
3 Make it personal. You may not be able to respond to every customer letter or call yourself, but avoid sending out anodyne letters that sound as if they were composed by robots. Nobody likes receiving the 'thank you for your input, it will be dealt with appropriately' response.

Find out your faults

The problem

The president of a medium-sized construction-supply company wanted to find out how he could improve his service to his customers.

The strategy

Initially he asked his major customers, with no useful results. Then he tried asking former clients who had complained about his service or had switched to different suppliers. He sent out ten invitations on company letterhead, asking them to meet to discuss how his company could serve them better. Nobody accepted – not surprisingly, since his invitation sounded like a sales pitch.

Finally, a management consulting firm, Alternative Visions, suggested a different approach: a more formal invitation to a gourmet lunch, with a $300 honorarium. On each invitation, the president added a handwritten note: 'Where else do you get wined, dined, and paid to tell me why I'm an ass?'

The outcome

Five of the former customers attended, and the president was quoted as saying, 'That was the hardest and most informative day of my career.' Based on the feedback, he overhauled his business and increased his revenues.

The lessons

Customers who are only too eager to tell their friends about their bad experiences with a business may not be so forthcoming when asked by the business itself. However, their complaints may be extremely valuable, so it is worth doing something different to motivate them to let you know what, in their view, you have done wrong.

Questions to ask yourself

1 Are you familiar enough with the aspects of your business that turn off some of your customers?
2 Are you willing to listen to criticism of your business?
3 Do you have a mechanism for gathering such criticism?

Tips: Finding your faults

1 First, keep a list of disgruntled customers or those who don't come back after having dealt with you previously.

2 Second, as in our example, find a way to make it enjoyable for them to criticise you.

3 Finally, if you feel that you would be too upset to hear the criticism, or couldn't do it without getting defensive, have someone else represent the company at the meeting.

Make that call, send that letter

The problem

Chris Roberts, a games creator, needed money – big money – to start his own company, Digital Anvil.

The strategy

Roberts's director of operations, Eric Peterson, suggested sending an email to the richest man in the world, Bill Gates.

The outcome

Not only did the email get through to Bill Gates, but the Microsoft mogul agreed to finance Roberts's games development and to give him full creative control. While the company will not release exact figures, an educated guess is that Microsoft has invested at least $50 million in Digital Anvil.

The lessons

Certainly Roberts's track record had a lot to do with Bill Gates's faith in him – Roberts was the one of the prime movers behind the hugely successful Wing Commander flight-simulation games while he was vice-president of new technology at Origin Systems. Even so, he was doubtful that Gates would respond, much less give him millions upon millions of dollars of financial support. The lesson is simple – ask and you may receive. Don't ask, and you definitely won't.

Questions to ask yourself

1 Who aren't you asking for support or help because you are convinced they'd never respond?

2   Who haven't you thought of asking yet?

3   How can you get through to the people you want to ask for help?

Tips: Advanced asking techniques

1   Make a list of what you have already achieved that might impress the people you are approaching. People like Bill Gates get lots of crank letters and calls, so you need to show right away that you are someone who should be taken seriously.

2   Make a 'wish' list of people who you feel might be in a good position to help you, and who could benefit themselves in the process. One of the reasons that Bill Gates supported Chris Roberts is that Microsoft didn't have a major presence in the games and entertainment arena, and they needed someone like Chris Roberts to gain them entry into that field. It always has to be a win-win situation, and you need be very clear about their part of the win.

3   Get into a playful frame of mind and brainstorm the best way to approach these people. If you treat it as a game, you will not feel intimidated.

Curiosity kills the cat – and attracts the customer

How the basic human drives are satisfied has changed, but the drives themselves have not. One of the strongest is curiosity. If your marketing effort can make people curious about your product or service, you will take a giant step: from someone trying to force information on to people, to someone who is satisfying *their* desire to know more.

Seeing is buying

The problem

Karen and Michael Duke, who run Duke Chimney Services, wanted a way to help customers to see how good the customers' fireplaces would look after being renovated by the company.

The strategy

The Dukes take digital photos of the fireplace, or have the potential customers email them their own photos. Then they use Adobe PhotoDeluxe Business Edition to digitally manipulate the photos to show how the fireplace would look after it is overhauled.

The outcome

Karen Duke told *Inc.* magazine, 'I have 100% closing when I use this method.' Now about a quarter of their business comes from outside their normal business reach, via the Internet. In these cases, they ship the replacement fireplaces to the customers for local installation.

The lessons

When customers can see exactly how your product will look in their environment, they are much more likely to buy. In this case, the investment (the cost of the camera and software) was minimal, and the process has even allowed the business to expand beyond its former reach.

Questions to ask yourself

1 Is there a way you can help your potential customers to visualise the impact of your product or service?
2 Can new technology help you do this more effectively than you have been able to achieve in more traditional ways (brochures and catalogues, for instance)?
3 Is there a way also to also use this technology to extend your reach, either geographically or in terms of the types of customer you have traditionally served?

Tips: How to personalise your product or service

1 Make it about your customers, specifically. As in our case study, sometimes it is possible to show people how the product or service will impact them directly. Another example is the system that some hairdressers have that takes a digital photo of the customer, and then superimposes various hairstyles on her face so she can choose the one she finds most flattering. A dressmaker could do something similar, as could a jeweller. Interior decorators could also show customers how different drapes or carpets would look in a particular setting. Generally, this level of individualisation means you have to be able to take a digital photo or the customer has to be able to supply it.
2 Make it about the type of customer you're dealing with. For example, if a customer in the market for a suit tells you how tall he is and describes his body shape, you can provide him

with pictures of how a particular suit looks on someone with the same general appearance.

Can you keep a secret?

The problem

How to make the Ford Focus a bestselling vehicle among young buyers.

The strategy

Ford used several strategies to give the Focus an image that would appeal to young buyers: they lent 125 of the cars to trendsetters, they used rap-style poems in their radio ads, they portrayed young people in their ads. So far, so predictable (if also effective). But they also took an unusual step: they kept a very low profile about the success of the car, on the basis that young buyers like to feel that they're individualists, not part of a herd.

The outcome

The strategy has helped keep the car streaming out of showrooms. Within its first two years of life, it became one of the world's top sellers.

The lessons

We tend to think that success is something to brag about, that if we tell potential buyers how many other customers have already bought our product, that will be a plus. Much of the time, this is true. But not when we want buyers to feel that they are discovering something new or are buying something exclusive.

Questions to ask yourself

1   Do your most likely customers want the novelty of being pioneers, or the security of following the crowd?
2   If your customers like to feel like pioneers and individualists, yet your product becomes very popular, how can you keep a low profile about that success? How can you maintain a

sense of mystique about the product even after it has hit a mass market?

Tips: Making each customer feel special

1 Include an element of individuality. One reason the Cabbage Patch Dolls were such a huge hit in their time was that each doll came with a unique certificate of adoption.

2 Find your customers via niche advertising or niche publicity. Generally a company will try to find the largest audience possible at one time (such as by advertising in a mass-market publication). However, if a feeling of exclusivity is desirable, it is preferable to find them via a number of targeted specialist publications, giving each readership the impression that the product is geared exclusively to them.

3 Create the illusion of shortages. Whether or not there is a genuine shortage of a particular automobile, for example, creating a waiting list also brings about the feeling that customers are getting something special. Nightclubs often do the same thing by delaying the opening of their doors until there's a long queue, on the basis that passers-by will assume that whatever is happening inside must be worth waiting for.

Make it interactive

The problem

Maxine Clark wanted to create a toy store that would make buying toys (in this case the soft variety) a fun experience for children.

The strategy

Clark opened the Build a Bear Workshop, a store in which children create their own teddy bears and other soft toys. The child selects an unstuffed toy, which might be a bear, a cow or a frog, among others, and takes it to a machine that fills it with stuffing (supervised by a store employee). Then the child takes a little heart-shaped pillow from a box and is told to rub it, kiss it and make a wish before the heart is put into the toy and the animal is sewn closed. The children also fill in a birth certificate for the animal and give it a name, and they can then buy clothes and other accessories for it before taking it home.

The outcome

The first store, established in 1997, was such a success that the company has opened another 33, and total annual revenues are in the neighbourhood of £12 million. Clark hopes to have at least 250 Workshops by the year 2007, and has produced a tape and compact disc of teddy-bear-related songs.

The lessons

Clark knew that kids like doing things and would feel more attached to a toy they had helped make than to one that was simply plucked off a shelf. She was able to support this feeling further through having the child name the animal, fill in its birth certificate and clothe it any way the child wants. Interactivity works – and not just on the web.

Questions to ask yourself

1 Is there any way that you can increase the interactivity between your business and your customers?
2 Is there any way to add a dimension of entertainment to your business? Naturally this is not limited to child-related businesses: Nike use their NikeTown stores this way, and Sony use their flagship stores (like the one in the Metreon Center in San Francisco and in the Sony Centre in Berlin) this way as well.

Tips: How to involve your customers more

1 Give your customers an element of choice – or an apparent element of choice. For example, if you publish an e-bulletin, why not let customers decide among several editions of it, so that the one they receive will be most closely tailored to their needs or interests? If you have the resources to do so, you can

publish several editions that are distinctly different. If not, the differences may be cosmetic – but the recipient still feels he or she has been catered to individually.

2   Ask your customers for input via surveys or questionnaires. Some customers can't be bothered to fill them in, but others like the idea that their opinions are valued.

3   If you do solicit customers' opinions, acknowledge their input and, if possible, let them know a specific change that will be made in line with their preferences.

Grab their attention

The problem

David Merrick, owner of the Cincinnati Coffee Company, was moving into new premises during the summer, traditionally the slowest season for selling coffee. He had to come up with new and inexpensive ways of attracting customers.

The strategy

Merrick joined with his store manager and a copywriter to brainstorm ideas. They came up with the notion of creating a soap opera about coffee, which they called *Days of Our Latte*. Every week, he posted a new chapter of the soap on a large outdoor sign located on a busy corner next to his store.

The outcome

Customers started coming in not only to buy coffee and sandwiches, but also to chat about the funny characters and storylines of the soap.

The lessons

Capturing customers' attention need not be expensive. This is a perfect case of a do-it-yourself approach that cost no money but was different enough to be effective. It made a mundane task – buying a coffee – more enjoyable, and customers yearn for a bit of entertainment during their working day.

Questions to ask yourself

1 Is there a way to add a bit of fun or entertainment to what you are offering customers?
2 What media are at your disposal? In this case, all that was needed was an outdoor sign that the shop already owned but had not been utilising very effectively.
3 Can you come up with something that is an ongoing feature, so that it will not only entertain customers but also bring them back?

Tips: Bringing in customers

1 Brainstorm a list of things that people enjoy. These could include soap operas, comics, magazines, music, theatre, sports and snacks. List as many as possible.
2 Now try combining those with the elements of your business to see which of the combinations give you ideas you could use. If you have a retail outlet, this might give you notions for displays, design elements or signage. If you communicate with your customers via a catalogue, it might give you inspiration for adding a fun element to that.

Go directly to the customer

The problem

A gardening service called the Lawn Jockey wanted to find new customers without spending much money.

The strategy

The company printed 28-by-20cm signs that they stick in lawns that look as if they could use some help. One of the signs says, in large letters, KEEP OFF GRASS. The fine print at the bottom reads, 'Once you give us a call, you'll never have to set foot on your lawn again. We mow. We trim. We mulch. And, of course, we beat any price. Lawn Jockey [and the phone number].'

The outcome

Using the signs doubled the Lawn Jockey's business in two months.

The lessons

Seeing these little signs sprouting on their lawns aroused the curiosity of the customers and gave them an immediate solution to their problem. At the same time, the company didn't disturb potential customers by ringing their doorbells and interrupting their day or evening. A few customers may have been annoyed by the signs, although the Lawn Jockey didn't register any complaints. If we use humour, and target our messages carefully, generally customers don't mind a bit of cheekiness.

Questions to ask yourself

1 Can you come up with a way to reach your customers directly without disturbing them?
2 Are you using humour to reach people?

Tips: Going to the customers

1 Brainstorm ways that you can target your customers and reach them more directly. In the case of our example, it was the lawns that revealed the need for the services of a gardener. Is there anything about your customers or their premises that make it obvious they might be in the market for your product or service?
2 Brainstorm ways that you can use humour to attract customers. In most cases, humour makes customers feel good about your business, as long as it is not offensive. If you're not particularly funny or witty, it's easy enough to hire a writer or cartoonist to do some of the work for you. Consider how you could inject humour into your printed materials, packaging, the signage of retail locations, even the uniforms worn by staff members.
3 Consider how you might make potential customers more curious about what it is you have to offer. Among the many

things that attract people are contests, quizzes, unusual window displays and unusual signs.

Give them the message

The problem

Louis Cocozza, a sales representative for a printing company, wanted to find a way to get in to see five particular potential customers who were not returning his calls.

The strategy

He bought a product called 'message in a bottle', a small bottle with an address label on the cork. A message can be put inside and, with the addition of two stamps, the bottle is deliverable by the Post Office. He wrote a note to each of the five elusive customers, saying, 'I've been trying to reach you for a long time, but I've been unsuccessful. As a last resort I've cast this note into the sea of mail, hoping my luck will change.'

The outcome

The next time he rang, four of the five took his call. Three of them agreed to see him and became customers. One of them became one of his very best customers.

The lessons

Cocozza used the curiosity factor. Yes, it's a gimmick but, at a time when a lot of businesses don't really offer much differentiation in price and level of service, it's important to stand out any way you can. Another curiosity-tickling strategy Cocozza uses is to send potential customers blank cards called 'puzzle notes'. He writes on them that he would like to have the chance to solve the potential customer's printing puzzles, then breaks the note up into fifteen jigsaw pieces. Most recipients can't resist putting the puzzle together to see what it says, and when he rings to follow up they generally agree to see him.

Questions to ask yourself

1 Are your written communications arousing the curiosity of your potential customers?
2 Can you think of a way of adapting Cocozza's two techniques to your own requirements?

Tips: Getting your message across

1 Brainstorm a list of all the types of things that make people curious. Certainly a jigsaw puzzle is one; others include a mysterious message, fortune cookies, crossword puzzles and word games.
2 For each of the above, brainstorm how you might use such a device to add a curiosity factor to some aspect of your marketing.

■ Hire a dog

The problem

When David Wase opened a framing store in a new city, he needed a way to get to know the local people and make it enjoyable for them to deal with him.

The strategy

Wase made a habit of walking around the neighbourhood with his dog, Taos, an eighty-pound Alsatian/Rottweiler mix, who, despite his fierce looks, was gentle as a lamb. He put a pouch around the dog's neck and, when curious passers-by stop to chat about the dog, Wase invites them to reach into the dog's pouch, which contains his (the dog's) business card. The canine's title is 'studio assistant'. Wase also gives the dog the run of the framing shop.

The outcome

Wase reports that the dog is a great conversation starter. Once they realise what a sweetheart Taos is, customers often bring in their children to play with him while having a picture framed, and others bring in their own dogs to play with the friendly 'studio assistant'. The shop's revenues have increased every year.

The lessons

As amazing as the technological revolution has been, people still crave the personal touch. Whenever you find a way to connect with people on a personal level, you increase your chances of creating a long-time customer.

Questions to ask yourself

1   If it's appropriate for your business, might a pet of some kind be a draw that attracts customers?
2   If a pet is not appropriate, what might be other conversation starters that would get people to ask about your business?

Tips: Arousing their curiosity

1   Begin by brainstorming a list of what kinds of things encourage people to talk to strangers. These might include pets, as in our example, shared hobbies, the weather, unusual items of clothing, what someone is reading, badges with unusual sayings, and unusual window displays. See how many more you can generate.
2   Go over the list of conversation starters you've come up with and consider whether and how each of them could be put to work to arouse people's curiosity about your business. For example, some years ago a multilevel-marketing company selling diet supplements issued each of their salespeople a badge that read, 'I lost [X] pounds! Ask me how!' Each rep filled in the number of pounds he or she had lost using the supplements, and the badges were extremely successful in opening conversations (admittedly, this was in the United States, where people are much quicker to chat with strangers).

People are bored with the usual – give them something different

You can lure people by arousing their curiosity, but the best way to keep them interested is to offer them something different. Of course the 'do something different' theme underlies most of the other principles, but it is also a principle in its own right. We are getting more and more jaded about advertising and publicity. You have to figure out a way to come at us from a different direction, to make the buying experience a (pleasant) surprise.

What's your USP?

The problem

American Rob Albert was looking for a product that would be a real stand-out. At the time of his breakthrough, he was selling horse shampoo to feed and tack stores, and not having a lot of financial success.

The strategy

It was when Albert heard that some customers were using the horse shampoo on their own hair that the light came on. It made sense: shampoo that successfully deals with the tangles in the coarse hair of manes should be able to handle the most troublesome human hair as well. That became the product's USP (Unique Selling Proposition).

The outcome

With this USP, Albert was able to get incredible amounts of free publicity (almost five hundred newspaper articles). He sold over $30 million worth of the product before he sold the company in order to move on to other ventures.

The lessons

In today's incredibly crowded marketplace, a product has to have an angle, a Unique Selling Proposition, to be noticed. If there's an angle that captures the attention of the press, half your work is done.

Questions to ask yourself

1 Does your product or service have a Unique Selling Proposition that sets it apart from the competition? If not, can you give it one?
2 Does your product or service have a story that could interest the press? If not, can you invent one that is credible and ethical?
3 When you hear an interesting bit of information about how people are using your product or service (as when Rob Albert heard that some of his customers were using the horse shampoo on their own scalps), do you stop to think of any possible marketing implications it may have?

Tips: How to stand out

1 One USP could be a product's unusual source. In your product, are the ingredients exotic? Has it been used in some different way? Was it invented by someone interesting or distinctive?
2 Another possibility is an unusual design. As we've seen with the Apple iMacs, the new Volkswagen Bug and the Chrysler PT Cruiser, a distinctive design can have a huge impact in the marketplace.

3 Another option is an unusual advertising mascot. Many products have caught on at least in part because they were represented by a unique character in their advertising and/or packaging (examples include the Energiser Bunny, the Jolly Green Giant and Tony the Tiger).

If everybody's got steak, add sizzle

The problem

Jim Kirchmeier, the owner of Classic Driving School, wanted to make his school more attractive to teenagers learning to drive.

The strategy

He bought a fleet of Porsches and had his instructors give lessons in them.

The outcome

His driving school became a huge success, and, after his first year, Kirchmeier doubled his fleet of Porsche 944s. As he pointed out, 'This is every kid's dream car.'

The lessons

When you figure out how to make a mundane product or service special, the customers will flock to your business.

Questions to ask yourself

1 What change in your product or service would make it stand out from the usual?
2 What change would make your product or service 'every customer's dream?'

Tips: How to make your product or service special

1 Do some creative daydreaming: in an ideal world, what would your customers want from you? For example, people who use tax accountants might wish for a process that makes it easy for them to collect their financial records

throughout the year and hand them over when it's tax time. People who take their cars to be repaired might wish for a clean, friendly environment in which the mechanics explain exactly what they need to do and give accurate estimates of when the work will be done. People who are looking for a new home might wish to see only those that fit the specifications they give and to have full information about the neighbourhoods in which the homes are located.

2 Brainstorm how these dreams might become realities. For example, an accountant might send clients a monthly package of envelopes in which receipts can be stored; a car repair shop could use a top private hospital as a model for redesigning the premises and scheduling appointments; an estate agent could offer video tours of appropriate homes, and offer a neighbourhood profile that includes information about local schools, hospitals, businesses and restaurants.

3 Try out your new ideas on a few of your current customers. Actually test the ideas in practice, or at least ask your customers how they'd like these changes if you were able to implement them.

Oaks from acorns

The problem

In 1980, the producer/director/writer John Cherry was trying to come up with a character to help promote an amusement park in Bowling Green, Kentucky.

The strategy

Cherry invented a character called Ernest, a loud-mouthed but likable working-class kind of a guy who put his nose into everybody's business, especially that of his fictional neighbour, Vern. Cherry hired a character actor named Jim Varney to play the part. Ernest's catchphrase was 'Hey, Vern!'

The outcome

Ernest was a hit. He starred in almost 4,000 adverts. But it went further than that – much further than John Cherry had ever dreamed. In 1985, Jim Varney as Ernest took part in the half-time show at the Indianapolis 500 races. The crowd of half a million cheered and clapped and screamed out, 'Hey, Vern!' In the audience were two Disney executives, Michael Eisner and Jeffrey Katzenberg. They were amazed at this response to the regional hero and signed him up. Ernest went on to star in four feature films for the Disney Studios and for a time had his own Saturday morning television programme.

The lessons

Just inventing the character of Ernest was doing something different. Giving him a memorable catchphrase was also a good idea. But another lesson is that sometimes, when we are creative, the success we have goes far beyond the boundaries we imagine. In this case, the presence of the two Disney executives was the serendipitous event that allowed Ernest to spread his wings and gain fame and fortune for his inventor and the actor who played him. Some might say that was luck, but, as someone once observed, 'The harder I work, the luckier I am.' In this case, John Cherry and Jim Varney developed the character, kept exposing him to the world, and looked for opportunities for him to be seen by more and more people, and that was the hard work that opened the door for luck as well.

Questions to ask yourself

1 Are you thinking big enough about your promotional activities?
2 Are you making sure that your promotional activities are reaching an ever-larger group of people?

Tips: Breaking boundaries

1 Brainstorm ways you can make your business more memorable. Something like a mascot or a character for a logo might be useful.

2   If these catch on, consider other ways you might take advantage of your invention. Could it lend itself to being the basis for a book, a toy, a calendar or any other spin-off?

3   It can work in reverse, too. If someone else has already come up with a popular or promising character that might fit your business well, you can negotiate the rights to it, or work out some kind of mutually beneficial arrangement.

Make it a show

The problem

Harold Ruttenberg, founder and CEO of Just for Feet, a chain of shoe stores, wanted to make it fun for his customers to come to his stores.

The strategy

Each of the 84 Just for Feet superstores is full of playful elements that appeal to adults and children. They include an indoor basketball court, a wall of video screens, a hot dog restaurant and laser light shows. Ruttenberg has said, 'We take our cue from Walt Disney, a master at making people smile.'

The outcome

When the firm went public in 1993, it was grossing $23 million; four years later it was grossing $500 million.

The lessons

Just for Feet makes an event of buying shoes – and a happy, playful event at that. Ruttenberg has said that his whole goal is to make customers happy to be in his shops despite the fact that they are there to give him their money. Being able to turn the shopping experience into one enjoyed by the entire family can have an enormous payoff.

Questions to ask yourself

1   How could you make the experience of dealing with your business more appealing or entertaining for your customers?

2 If it's appropriate, how could you make your business location attractive to the entire family?

Tips: Making it entertaining

1 Brainstorm whether and how the example of Walt Disney might hold any lessons for your business.

2 Consider other models as well, from a variety of businesses such as McDonald's, the TGIF restaurant chain, the Nike superstores, the Sony showcase centres and others, to determine whether any of them might give you clues as to how to make your business into more of an entertainment experience.

3 If you don't have a retail location, consider whether it would be appropriate to make your materials, such as your letterhead, business cards, brochures and fliers, more playful and entertaining.

Cook up a winning combination

The problem

The owners of HomeChef, a chain of cooking schools and kitchen stores, wanted to find a way to attract customers even though large discount stores offer similar goods less expensively.

The strategy

Its founder, Judith Ets-Hokin, decided to create a total cooking environment and to offer customers free advice as well. The stores feature samples of freshly cooked food, free one-hour cooking demonstrations and salespeople who have been trained to answer a huge variety of cooking-related queries. On Thanksgiving Day, the company even provides a free hotline for customers who are having problems cooking the traditional turkeys.

The outcome

The chain has grown to a total of eight stores, with a gross of over $14 million.

The lessons

Price is not necessarily the most important thing. If you can create a shopping environment that makes people feel at home and adds value to the shopping experience with advice, demonstrations and samples, the customers will come even if the products on offer cost a bit more. Knowledgeable salespeople, often a rare commodity, can also be important in creating customer loyalty.

Questions to ask yourself

1 If you have a retail space, how can you make shopping there more of an experience?
2 Are your salespeople knowledgeable enough to form a bond with your customers?
3 How do you add value to the shopping experience for your customers?

Tips: Attracting customers

1 Ask yourself what problems your customers have in relation to the products you are offering. In our example, customers may find certain kinds of dishes difficult to prepare; they may need help finding exotic ingredients; and they may need advice on how to use certain kinds of kitchen tools.
2 Brainstorm how you might help customers cope with some of these problems. Could you offer free informational fliers or booklets? Could you have in-store demonstrations? Could you give away or sell videos that offer useful information? Could you have salespeople adept at answering specialised questions? Could you operate a hotline?

Everybody loves a freebie

Giving potential customers something for free in the hope that they will then go on to buy something is not a new strategy. However, it's one that is gaining more importance because it's used so much on the Internet. Sites offer information or entertainment for free. For large sites, the number of visitors makes it possible to charge advertisers to display banners or other ads. Most sites, though, will survive only if the customer buys something from them after being lured there by the free stuff. Similarly, many companies give away basic software programs, hoping that buyers will choose to upgrade for a fee. If you can hook people with something that's free, you will have a powerful marketing approach.

Give it the personal touch

The problem

Mary Lou Fox, CEO of Westhaven Corp, an American company that supplies medical services to nursing homes, wanted to get nursing home administrators to consider using her company, but most of them threw away anything they considered advertising material.

The strategy

For her first direct-mail piece, Fox used a strategy that had worked for her in soliciting donations for a charity: she hand-addressed the letters, making them look like personal correspondence. She also enclosed a fifty-cent lottery ticket, along with the question, 'Do you want to be a winner?' This caught the attention of the recipients, and gave them something to associate with her name when she called them to follow up. It also gave her a conversational opener for the follow-up calls: 'Did you win?'

The outcome

None of the recipients won, but most of them did take her phone calls, which gave her the foot in the door that she needed.

The lessons

We are all bombarded by so much junk post that the personal touch stands out. By using the lottery tickets, Fox also took advantage of two basic human traits: curiosity and the desire to get something for nothing. Even when the recipients didn't win, they probably associated her calls with a sense of fun.

Questions to ask yourself

1 What are the usual ways you use to contact potential customers? Is there a way of making these efforts more personal or more interesting?
2 How could you make people curious about your business?
3 How could you take advantage of people's desire to get something for nothing?

Tips: Using the personal touch

1 As in the case study, hand-address envelopes. You don't need to do this yourself, of course: you can hire students or home workers, and pay them per envelope.
2 Enclose something that will intrigue the recipients. In the case study it was a lottery ticket, but other examples might be a quiz, a limerick with the last line missing (so they have

to supply it themselves), or a fortune cookie with your advertising message inside.

3 Use a feature that will make the mailing memorable and give you an opening for follow-up phone calls: 'I'm the one who sent you the catalogue in the furry envelope,' or 'I'm the one who sent you his business card inside the bottle.' Naturally it is best if you can make this unusual feature tie in directly to the nature of your business, but (as in the case study) the connection doesn't have to be that strong.

Surround the target

The problem

An author wanted to appear on *The Tonight Show* with Johnny Carson to promote his book. However, it was America's most popular late-night show, and the competition to get on to it was intense.

The strategy

Whereas most authors and agents would have sent the book to the programme's producer or to the star, this writer obtained a list of all the people on the programme's staff and sent each of them a copy. Soon a lot of people were walking around with the book in their hands and talking about it.

The outcome

The show's host, Johnny Carson, noticed the book everywhere and asked for a copy of it himself. Intrigued not only by the book but by the author's clever ploy, Carson invited him to be a guest on the show.

The lessons

Sometimes the best way to get to someone is to surround them. While Carson and his producer received literally hundreds of books, the staff members never did. Therefore, it was likely that they'd be intrigued, that they'd at least sample the book, and that they'd talk about it. That meant there was a good chance it would come to the attention of the two main players as well.

Questions to ask yourself

1 If you can't get to a person you'd like to influence in some way, who can you get to that is around this person?
2 What would be the best way to reach these people?

Tips: Reaching by surrounding

1 Remember that the 'gatekeepers' – secretaries, personal assistants, security guards and so forth – seldom get any attention. If you send them a sample product, for example, it will make a much bigger impression than it makes on a buyer who receives such things all the time. Think about what you can send the gatekeepers that they will like and that will prompt them to talk about your business. We're not talking about bribery here, but rather getting some tangible representation of your business into their hands.
2 Find the best delivery system for getting it to them. The ideal is to send it to them at their workplace, so it is visible. If that's not possible, can you have someone hand it out as they go into their office or factory in the morning? If not, can you find a local pub or café where many of them hang out at lunchtime, and do it there?
3 Allow the process to work by itself. If you push too hard, people will be annoyed and the scheme may backfire.

What else can you sell?

The problem

The American network NBC, facing higher programme costs and declining market share, wanted to find additional sources of revenue.

The strategy

NBC aired a miniseries called *The '60s* and during it made on-air announcements of a special toll-free number viewers could ring to order a CD of the music from the programme.

The outcome

The network sold over 35,000 units (at $29.95 each) over the air and will earn more from sales in retail outlets. The week the miniseries was on the air, the CD went from number 87 to 65 in the album charts of the music magazine *Billboard*. NBC executives have stated that the potential for merchandising is having an influence on their selection of the programmes they will air.

The lessons

There are often unexploited opportunities for spin-off merchandising. Going back to our example, when NBC offered viewers a direct way of ordering videocassettes of the miniseries *Merlin*, they sold over 100,000 units. In both cases, they made it easy for the customers to make an impulse buy via a toll-free number. In the future, the Internet may also be an important channel for such purposes.

Questions to ask yourself

1 In your business, is there the potential for a spin-off product that you could offer?
2 How can you make it easier for customers to buy these auxiliary goods?

Tips: Finding new things to sell

1 On a large sheet of paper, write the name of your existing product or service in a circle in the middle. Branching out from it in all directions, jot down the names of any related items or services. Ask a few colleagues to add more, so you have as many items as possible.
2 Now circle any of the related words that suggest a practical spin-off product. For example, a restaurant could sell

cookbooks, a pet shop could offer videotapes on how to take care of the type of animal being purchased, and a store selling watches could offer accessories (such as cufflinks or brooches) that match the faces of the watches.

3   For each, brainstorm the best way to make it easy for your customer to buy the associated product. In a restaurant, the cookbook could be bought immediately; in a pet shop the video tape could also be held in stock. In the case of accessories to a wristwatch, perhaps these would be ordered at the time the watch is bought, but then made individually by an artist and delivered later.

The power of samples

The problem

Mike Taggett wanted to market Chums, a line of adjustable eyewear retainers especially for sport. The problem was that he had very little money.

The strategy

Taggett used what money he did have to buy a booth at the Las Vegas Snow Show, figuring that his product would have great appeal for specs-wearing skiers. He asked a friend to circulate around the show handing out free samples.

The outcome

One of the people who took free samples turned out to be a representative of Swatch, the watch company. He wore the pink Chums and got so many compliments and comments that he realised the product could be a trendy hit. Swatch placed an order for 300,000 Chums. The company has since added a line of sportswear, and its products are sold in over twenty countries.

The lessons

If a sample falls into the right hands, the effect can be tremendous. There's no better way for people to appreciate the product than to try it for themselves, and no better way to get them to try it than to give it to them for free.

Questions to ask yourself

1 Are you handing out enough samples? If your product is too expensive to hand out, can you give demonstrations of what it can do?
2 Are you handing out samples at the right places? In our case study, there is no way Taggett could predict exactly who would try out the samples, but he did know that the people attending the show were a good target audience.

Tips: Making samples work for you

1 Who would you like to make familiar with your product or service? Make a list of all the groups that come to mind.
2 Where are you likely to find those people? Again, make as comprehensive a list as possible.
3 Brainstorm how you can get samples (or demonstrations) to these people. This might include taking a stand at a trade show, as in our example, or doing a targeted mailing, or sponsoring an event that will attract the right kinds of people, or making a samples offer in a publication that is read by your target group.

Give them praise and baubles

The problem

When Napoleon took power, he needed ways to win the loyalty and dedication of his military leaders.

The strategy

Napoleon devised an elaborate system of medals and other honours. 'Baubles?' he said once. 'It is with baubles that men are led … You imagine that an army is defeated by analysis? Never. In a republic, soldiers performed great deeds through a sense of honour.

It was the same under Louis XIV.' He came up with the Légion d'Honneur, and he invented the golden eagles at the top of flagstaffs, whose capture by the enemy was to be avoided at any cost.

The outcome

The system of rewards Napoleon established worked well at motivating his military leaders, and even the ordinary foot soldiers. He created an image of glory that helped keep him in power.

The lessons

Compliments, awards and honours have always worked well and continue to work well in motivating and rewarding people. The fact that royal awards continue to be coveted at a time when other aspects of the monarchy have gone out of favour is testament to this. So is the satisfaction that salespeople get from being named Salesperson of the Month. Best of all, these prizes are free.

Questions to ask yourself

1 Are you using these kinds of award to motivate your employees?
2 Are you using awards that make your customers feel special?
3 Are you using awards to get publicity for your company?

Tips: Reward them with awards

1 Make a list of the performance objectives you have for your employees. What kind of behaviour would you like to see more of? That's the kind of behaviour that you need to reward, and it doesn't have to be with expensive prizes. Often a public commendation is enough.
2 What kind of behaviour do you want to see more of from your customers? For example, do you want more referrals, repeat orders, and testimonials? Find ways to reward your customers with awards, too. If there can be an Employee of the Month, why not have a Customer of the Month?

Add value

The problem

Back in 1888, people found loading and unloading film into cameras as daunting as most of us find programming video recorders these days.

The strategy

George Eastman ran an ad that read, 'You press the button – we do the rest.' His first camera came with the film already loaded, and, when customers finished the roll of film, they took the camera back to the lab. There, technicians removed the film, substituted a new one and returned the camera along with the developed photos.

The outcome

This procedure sounds ridiculously unwieldy to us now, but it had the desired effect: it made the new phenomenon of taking your own pictures as simple as possible. The freebie in this case was the service. Once people were used to taking their own pictures, they learned to remove and insert film as well. Kodak dominated the camera and film markets for decades, and is still one of the major players.

The lessons

If you have a new product or service, one that may intimidate customers, it is well worth your while to add anything that can make the process easier for them.

Questions to ask yourself

1 Is there any aspect of your business or service that people might find intimidating or confusing?
2 If so, what could you do to make it easier for them?

Tips: Adding value

1 To determine whether any aspect of your business is confusing or intimidating, bring in outsiders, ideally people

who have never dealt with this kind of business before. They will see things that you would overlook because you know the process too well. Pay particular attention to their questions.

2   Consider each part of your customer's experience with your business (this might include placing an order, phoning for help or making a complaint) and determine whether there is any way you can add value by making it simpler or providing additional help.

Discounts that count

The problem

Mike Friedman, the owner of a pizza restaurant, wanted to come up with a more effective way to use discount coupons to bring customers into his establishment.

The strategy

Instead of printing up the usual discount-coupon fliers, Friedman switched to adhesive ones that resemble delivery notices (like Post-it notes). Because they can be stuck to fridges or phones, they are less likely to get lost.

The outcome

The response rate to the usual types of fliers is 1 to 3 per cent. The sticky coupons generated a 30-per cent response rate. After a year of use, the coupons were still generating a 20-per cent response rate.

The lessons

Most advertising material is thrown away, so any way you can find to make yours more likely to be kept is worth exploring.

Questions to ask yourself

1   Are you using discount coupons to give your customers the feeling that they are getting something extra? Even if you are

not in a business for which such coupons are used routinely, might they be a good idea?

2 If you do use discount coupons, are they in a form that is likely to get a good response?

Tips: Using coupons for results

1 Brainstorm how coupons might work in your business. The obvious use is to give a percentage discount on the price of a product or service, but they could also give people a bonus, a prize if they frequent your business a certain number of times; or they might give them a discount to another business, if you set up a co-operative arrangement. For example, a flower shop might give discount coupons for wine purchased at a nearby off-licence, and the off-licence might hand out discount coupons for flowers bought at the flower shop.

2 Brainstorm how you can help ensure that your coupons won't get lost or thrown away quickly. For example, a coupon could be attached to a calendar or to a mini-poster.

Give them a mirror

The problem

The owners of Amsterdam's local newspaper *Het Parool* wanted to increase their subscriptions and reader loyalty.

The strategy

They asked each new subscriber to send them a passport-size photograph of themselves. They turned each photo into a transfer and heat-sealed them on to the sides of two of the city's trams.

The outcome

There was a surge in subscriptions and people enjoyed looking for their photos on the sides of the trams. It gave people a tiny version of their 'fifteen minutes of fame'.

The lessons

There is no one we find quite as fascinating as ourselves. Any business that takes advantage of our interest in ourselves, especially as a free bonus, will win friends – and new customers.

Questions to ask yourself

1   Is there some way that you make your customers feel special?
2   Can you think of some ways that you could appeal to the customers' vanity or self-interest in a way that makes them feel good about doing business with you?

Tips: Making them feel special

1   Start by brainstorming a list of ways that *you* have been made to feel special. Don't restrict yourself to business contexts – in general, what makes you feel good? This might include getting compliments, receiving small gifts or seeing your name in print.
2   With the list in hand, brainstorm how each of these might translate to something that your business could do to make your customers feel good.

Sneak up on them

The problem

The Duncan Yo-Yo company wanted to make sure their toy could compete with the electronic gizmos that kids love these days.

The strategy

The company managed to persuade more than two thousand middle schools to include the toy in their curricula. They provide the toys at cost, and give teachers physics lesson plans that incorporate the yo-yos.

The outcome

The yo-yo has become popular again, and the teachers were grateful for the help with their lessons. After three years of the school distribution, yo-yo sales shot up by 400 per cent.

The lessons

The company doesn't make any profit on the yo-yos it distributes to schools, but it does awaken the children's awareness of the toys, and it's likely that they graduate to more expensive models. Also, those children who are not in the classes that get the yo-yos will see the toys in use and want them as well. If you can get a segment of your target audience to use your product and be seen to be using it, often that creates demand among others.

Questions to ask yourself

1   If you could get any group to use your product, and be seen to be using it, what group would that be?
2   Have you considered innovative ways to get your product to that group, even if it means doing so at cost or at a loss?

Tips: Getting it into their hands

1   Brainstorm who are the types of people who, by using your product or service, would influence others to want it as well.
2   Using that list, brainstorm how you could best get them as customers or clients. Can you give them a free sample? Can you tie distribution to a credible entity such as a school, church, or charity?

Consider the eye of the beholder

The customer's perception of you is at least as important as what you are really like. The image you project includes your paper image (business cards, letterheads, brochures), the image of your store or office, and your personal image. First you must think about the appropriate image for your product, service, and business, then how to convey it. If the image you have currently does not attract customers, change it.

Jumping into the web

The problem

Walter Geer realised that his promotional-products company didn't stand out in any way from its competitors, and therefore was unlikely ever to break out from the pack.

The strategy

Geer decided to transform his company into an Internet-only business (www.ecompanystore.com). This meant losing most of his existing customers (he didn't feel he had the resources to keep his original business going and also expand to the web), and investing in the construction of an effective website and promoting it so potential customers would know about it.

The outcome

After a few months with no revenues, business started to pick up. Geer told *Entrepreneur* magazine, 'The Internet let us move from being a small company to a national player.' Being on the Internet has allowed the company to win large accounts that never considered doing business with it before.

The lessons

Sometimes re-evaluating the nature of your business and being willing to risk everything to operate in a new way pays off. In this case, Walter Geer realised that the Internet was dramatically changing the nature of business-to-business purchases.

It's also important to know how thinly you can spread yourself and still be effective. In this instance, Geer decided that trying to keep his traditional business going and also making a major entry into the Internet would overtax his resources. Trying to do too many things may mean you don't do any of them well enough to have a major impact in your field.

Questions to ask yourself

1 What is the impact of the Internet on your type of business?
2 Might you be better off going to an Internet-only operation?
3 Do you have the resources to pursue that strategy?
4 Are you confident enough of the potential of this strategy to risk losing at least some of your existing customers?

Tips: How to determine whether your business is right for the Internet

1 Do a search to find out which websites already exist that offer your type of product or service. If there is already an Internet market leader in your category, you'll have to find a way to distinguish yourself from it. For a while, the conventional wisdom was that it was worth any amount of money to be first in; this has been proven to be wrong, but it's still the case that latecomers have to offer something different and ideally better.

2   Consider the impact of delivery charges. One site that was offering discounted vitamins and other health-related goods went out of business when customers proved unwilling to place small orders because the postage and handling fees often added a good 50 per cent to the cost of the order.

3   Consider how you will get people to your website. Many Internet businesses started with huge amounts of investment capital that they spent on traditional advertising to make customers aware of their site. If you don't have such resources, you'll have to come up with guerrilla techniques for luring customers to your site.

You can fool some of the people some of the time

The problem

A new American advertising agency was about to fail in its first year.

The strategy

The ad agency belonged to Jerry Della Femina, who later became one of the legends of the advertising world. But he had few clients and it looked like the company was going to go broke after only a year. He decided to take a huge risk. He spend all of his remaining money, $3,000, on a huge Christmas party (this was back when $3,000 was worth perhaps $50,000 in today's terms).

He sent out a thousand invitations to journalists, potential clients, even to his competitors. Years later, he recalled, 'People kept coming up to me that night, saying, "You know, I heard that things weren't going so good, but, boy, you've got a place here, haven't you?" And we said, "Things are going great, man."'

The outcome

The party had the desired effect. Wanting to be part of such an obviously successful new venture, several clients signed up immediately, and the agency went on to great success.

The lessons

In many businesses, how potential customers perceive you is at least as important as the reality. This is probably even truer than it was when Della Femina threw his party. People love to be associated with success, while the whiff of trouble or failure puts them off. To breed success, appear successful.

Naturally the image people associate with success varies according to the kind of business you are in. They would not expect a successful artist to have the same success indicators as a successful accountant, so it's up to you to decide what kind of image would be most appropriate for your line of business.

Questions to ask yourself

1   What kind of image are you projecting personally, and what kind of image does your business project? You are probably too close to these questions to answer them accurately yourself. Ask colleagues and friends to write down the four adjectives that come to mind when they think of you as a businessperson and when they think of your business. To encourage honesty, allow them to do this in writing and anonymously. If possible, do the same with a few customers – and a few people who have chosen not to do business with you.

2   What signs of success apply to your business or service? Are there ways you can project these signs?

Tips: Projecting the image of success

1   Make the most of your personal image. This includes your grooming, how you dress, the kind of vehicle you drive. Many of the larger clothing stores have in-house consultants who can help you develop a new look.

2   Make the most of your paper image: business cards, letterhead, brochures and fliers, packaging. If you've done much of this work yourself in the past, it may be worth investing in the services of a graphic designer to upgrade the look.

3 Consider the image of your office or store. Try walking into it with as free a mind as possible. What words come to mind to describe it? Efficient? Chaotic? Relaxed? Friendly? Cool? Old-fashioned?

4 Be sure that all three of these aspects of image are congruent. If they are contradicting each other, it's unlikely that you are projecting a clear, positive image.

Setting an example

The problem

Despite good reviews, audiences for Gian Carlo Menotti's opera *The Medium* were sparse.

The strategy

Menotti invited his old mentor, the famous conductor Toscanini, to go to the opera, hoping word of his attendance might encourage others to come.

The outcome

Fortunately, Toscanini liked the opera so much that he went a second night, and even a third. Toscanini was a revered but reclusive figure, and soon the gossip columns were all saying that, if you wanted to see him, go and see *The Medium*. People assumed that, if *he* liked the opera, it must be good. From that point on, the opera sold out seven nights a week.

The lessons

In every field, there are opinion leaders, people whose example others will follow. This, of course, is the reasoning behind employing celebrities to endorse products – even products about which they don't have any particular expertise. However, it's far more convincing (and less expensive) to get an endorsement (explicit, or, as in our example, implied) that is not paid for.

Questions to ask yourself

1 In your field, who are the opinion leaders?
2 How can you get them to use your product or service?
3 How can you make it known that they use your product or service?

Tips: Getting trendsetters to use your product or service

1 If yours is a local or regional business, the celebrities can be local or regional, too. They don't even need to be famous in the conventional sense. Within each field, whether it be accounting or zoology, there are people who are known and respected by their peers, even though they are not known to the public at large. Identify who these people are in your area.

2 Give these people an incentive to use your product or service. A good one is to give it to them for free, or at a discount. Don't assume this will not work if they are well-to-do. If you go to any convention or trade show, you will see CEOs who earn six-figure incomes queuing up for promotional goodies that cost a pound or two. We all like getting something for nothing.

3 Ask them for their opinion about your product or service. If they like it, ask whether you have their permission to quote them. If they say no, ask whether you can at least mention that they are your customers.

4 If appropriate, invite them to attend a charity fundraising event at your business. If they are famous, they may see this as another opportunity to maintain their public profile. If they are not famous, they will probably be flattered to be asked.

Judge a book by its cover

The problem

Books by Agatha Christie, traditionally extremely popular, stopped selling well.

The strategy

The publishers hired a market research firm to find out what was causing the problem. The answer turned out to be that the covers of the new editions of her works were too violent. They gave buyers the impression that these were horror books, not the kind of genteel mysteries that Christie wrote. Those who wanted mysteries didn't buy the books; those who did want gore were disappointed.

The outcome

The publisher changed the covers, and sales rose by 40 per cent.

The lessons

There are two lessons here. One is not to jump to conclusions about what is causing a lack of sales or other problem. It would have been easy to assume that Christie's kind of mysteries were considered too old-fashioned by modern readers, or that people were too busy watching TV detective programmes to read mysteries any more. Instead, the publishers did something very straightforward: they hired someone to ask customers.

The second lesson is that people do judge a book by its cover – in this case, literally, but of course that applies to all kinds of packaging. It even applies to the décor of a retail outlet, and certainly to the décor of bars and restaurants. It even applies to our individual way of dressing. It pays to be sure that the packaging of what we are offering is sending the right message to potential customers.

Questions to ask yourself

1 If you are having problems with any aspect of your business, who are the logical people to ask about the source of the problem?

2 What is the most effective way to ask these people for their input? Is it something you can do easily yourself, or would it make sense to hire an outside person or firm to do it for you?

3 What does your packaging say about your business? (Here we mean 'packaging' in the broadest sense, to include the

product, your premises, your signage, your business cards and letterhead, even how you and your employees dress.) Again, don't assume you know the answer to this – ask the customers.

4 If your packaging isn't reflecting your product or service accurately, how can you revamp it to better effect?

Tips: Finding out what's turning customers off

1 When people don't buy your product or service, ask them why. Naturally this has to be done in a non-aggressive way. One approach is to hand them a questionnaire and a stamped, self-addressed envelope and ask them to fill it in and post it to you. Tell them a token of your thanks is enclosed. If you enclose a pound, or a lottery ticket, or some other small item, they are far more likely to return the questionnaire.

2 Ask a colleague or friend to go through the same experience a customer would, whether this entails ordering an item from your company on the telephone, visiting your restaurant for a meal or whatever. Ask them to evaluate every part of the experience and give you their opinions. Many restaurants, hotels and chains of stores use 'mystery shoppers' or 'mystery guests' to do this, but there's no reason why a small business can't do the same thing less formally.

Look and feel the part

The problem

William Zanker was trying to get his agent to help him launch the Learning Annex, a programme of evening classes. The agent refused because in her opinion Zanker 'smelled cheap'. Astonished, he asked her what she meant. She explained that she was talking about his inexpensive suit, which gave totally the wrong impression. She gave him a challenge: spend $1,000 on a new suit, or find someone else to help him with his venture.

The strategy

Although Zanker had never spent more than $100 on a suit, he went along with the challenge and bought one for $1,000.

The outcome

Zanker told *Success* magazine, 'That suit was magical. When I wore it, I smelled powerful, I walked differently. As I started feeling more confident, The Learning Annex began to take off.'

The lessons

It's true that to some degree people judge us by how we dress and look, and the appearance of success instils confidence not only in ourselves but in others. Even so, the moral of the story isn't that we have to wear an expensive suit. In this case, the agent may have chosen the suit as a symbol of Zanker's lack of confidence and wisely predicted that spending that kind of money on himself would be a confidence booster.

The point is that, if we are trying to win over other people, we must project confidence in ourselves. For one person, an expensive suit or car may do the trick; for another it may be carrying a picture of a spouse who believes totally in that person. Whatever it takes to look and feel the part, do it.

Questions to ask yourself

1 What is the best look for the thing that you are trying to accomplish? What look would give you the most confidence?
2 Do you have that look?
3 If you don't have it, what would give it to you?

Tips: How to get the look – and the feeling

1 Put yourself in the place of your potential customer or client. What look would they consider most appropriate or inspiring? Is this a look with which you are comfortable? There is no one acceptable look for every person – there are successful entrepreneurs who dress like bankers, and

successful entrepreneurs who dress like poets. You just have to recognise that, if the look you adapt is not the expected one, you'll have to work harder to demonstrate to people that you are still the right person for them to deal with.

2 Do you have any clothes or accessories in which you feel particularly successful or confident? Make it a point to wear them. Is this superstition? Probably, but so what, if it works?

A rose by any other name

The problem

Gene Roddenberry wanted to sell the new, ground-breaking series *Star Trek* to a network, but had great difficulty doing this because the programme he had in mind was unlike anything else then on the air.

The strategy

Finally, he hit on the idea of changing his description of the series. To the people at NBC, he said the series would be like *Wagon Train* in space. (*Wagon Train* was a very successful western series on the air at the time.)

The outcome

He sold the series, and a legend was born, which has spawned films, additional television series, and millions upon millions of pounds of merchandising.

The lessons

Roddenberry realised that most people are uncomfortable with anything really new – particularly television executives, who tend to play it safe because their own careers are constantly on the line. So he linked an unknown element (a show about space) with a well-known, successful one, *Wagon Train*.

People respond best when a product or service is described to them in terms they understand. This is especially important when what is being proposed is new and different.

Questions to ask yourself

1 If your product or service is not accepted as easily as you think it should be, might the reason be that it is too new or different?
2 If so, do you need a new way to describe it?

Tips: Making it accessible

1 List the important attributes of the new product or service.
2 For each of the attributes, list one or more existing products or services to which the attribute applies.
3 Experiment with finding a way to express the key benefits by comparing the product to a combination of two or more that already exist. For example, a software program that learns your word-processing habits and makes your typing easier might be described as, 'the love child of Mavis Beacon and Einstein'. Or you might say it's 'like having Jeeves hiding inside your computer'.

Watch out for side effects

The problem

The tax-return preparation firm H & R Block found that their offices were very crowded at certain times of the day and wanted to establish a better flow of customers.

The strategy

They decided to allow customers to make appointments via telephone, as well as dropping in (up to this point, the system had not allowed for appointments, and if the office was crowded the person simply took a number and waited for his or her turn). The company instituted the new system in branches all over America at the same time.

The outcome

Customers were delighted to be able to make appointments – but those who were queuing for service were outraged to see other customers come in and be served ahead of them. Many of them walked out and never came back. The system has been changed so that phone appointments are taken only for those hours when drop-in traffic will predictably be low.

The lessons

The way this good new idea was implemented was a failure. Henry Bloch, co-founder of H & R Block, cited this as his biggest mistake in a feature in *Inc.* magazine, but also said it led to a larger lesson. 'The biggest lesson is,' he said, 'don't jump in and change something that's been working for years until you've tested it.' Sometimes the enthusiasm for what seems an obviously good idea overcomes prudence.

Questions to ask yourself

1 If you have new ideas you want to implement, have you considered adequately the effect they may have on existing parts of your business?
2 If you want to implement some new ideas, do you have a way of testing them first to see how well they work and whether they have any unintended side effects?

Tips: Catching problems early

1 When possible, do a simulation first. The hot topic these days is computer simulations of complex procedures, but a simulation can also be done simply, with people. If the new idea involves customers directly, do a role-play with colleagues or staff members pretending they are customers, and then try it out with selected customers.
2 Identify a way that the new idea can be implemented in part of your system. Depending on the idea, you may be able to limit it geographically (that is, try it out in one branch, or just one part of the company) or by time (that is, give it a trial period).

3   Don't look only to see whether it has the intended outcome (after all, the first version of the appointments system did help the flow of customers), but also keep your eyes open for effects you were not anticipating (in the example, that some of the flow of customers was out of the building, never to return).

Time is not money – it's more valuable than money

We have more and more demands put on our time, and the amount of time you have to capture the attention of your target audience is limited. In politics, sound bites have replaced debate; in advertising, the ten-second ad is now more common than the thirty-second one. You must find ways of getting attention *fast*.

From snore to score

The problem

Eddie Paul, an inventor, found that, when he tried to explain his new design for a pump compressor motor to potential buyers, they were tuning out from boredom before he could finish.

The strategy

Paul developed a sales presentation that uses graphics and animation to explain the device in under five minutes, using his laptop computer. Paul told the *New York Times*, 'This helps me to show my product in its best light – better than the pump itself, which I have to take apart to really demonstrate.'

The outcome

Using his new presentation, Paul won a licensing contract from the outboard-engine manufacturer Mercury Marine, and has deals pending with over twenty other companies.

The lessons

Your customer has to understand what you're offering – and the amount of time you have to convey the essence is shrinking. Even if your product or service isn't particularly complex, you still need to make clear quickly what is different and better about what you are offering. In this case, Paul used computer software and hardware to get his points across, but there are many other possibilities.

Questions to ask yourself

1 What are the key points your potential customers should know about your product or service?
2 How much time does it now take you to get these key points across?
3 How could you do it more quickly and more appealingly? Would it make sense to use other media (illustrations, animations, simple charts, audio tapes, for example)?

Tips: How to get your points across effectively

1 Limit yourself to three key benefits of the product or service (often one is enough).
2 Appeal to as many senses as possible. What information can you put into visuals, into speech, even into touch (for example, letting the potential customer handle the product)?
3 Be aware of the ever-diminishing attention span. Consider hooks you can use to capture the customers' attention. Once you have it, have a strategy for holding on to it (by adding surprising information, for instance, or by asking them questions or appealing to a different sense).

Let yourself be seen

The problem

The country singer Garth Brooks, then an unknown, wanted to

find success. All seven major record companies in Nashville rejected him.

The strategy

Brooks's manager, Bob Doyle, made him attend an audition evening at the Bluebird Café, which cost them $32.50. Doyle later recalled, 'Garth thought it was a waste of money. The second act on the bill didn't show, so I convinced them to let Garth go on early. He did two songs and nailed everybody to the wall …'

The outcome

A representative from Capitol Records offered them a contract right then and there. Brooks's debut album was an overnight success, and he went on to become the most successful country singer of all time.

The lessons

Bob Doyle knew that you must take all opportunities to expose yourself or your product or service to potential buyers. In this case, the right person heard Brooks at the right time doing the right song – a long shot, certainly, but one that paid off incredibly well.

Questions to ask yourself

1 If you're discouraged about the response to your idea/project/service, might you be only one more attempt away from success?
2 Are you putting your project or idea where those in a position to help you can see it?
3 What new ideas can you come up with for showcasing yourself or your project?
4 Are you willing to invest reasonable amounts of money to get the exposure you need?

Tips: Being seen by the right people

1 Start by identifying who the right people are. Make a list of all the kinds of people (as well as specific individuals) who could be in a position to help you.

2 Identify where these people are to be found. Obviously they have a work location, but where else might you come into contact with them? Possibilities include conventions, openings, social events, charity events and so on.

3 Develop a strategy for how to approach these people in an appropriate manner. For example, if you meet someone at a charity event, obviously it's not appropriate to go into a long sales pitch for your business. You would only introduce yourself, perhaps mention the name of your business, and follow up with a letter or fax to their business address the following day.

Make lemonade

The problem

Tegra Telephone Systems wanted to come up with a way to make customers *enjoy* being put on hold, rather than resent it.

The strategy

The company bought a machine that digitally loads and plays twelve minutes of information on a loop. Andy Dinkin, the company's president, loaded a sales tape he had recorded, featuring telephone marketing tips.

The outcome

The callers' feedback was uniformly positive – to the extent that some of them asked to be put back on hold to hear the rest of the tape.

The lessons

There's a saying: 'When life gives you lemons, make lemonade.' In other words, turn a disadvantage into an advantage. People resent wasting their time (one estimate is that heavy telephone users spend as much as an hour a week on hold). On the other hand, they enjoy being entertained or educated. The lesson is to take something that normally wastes their time and transform it into a positive experience (this principle could apply to situations in which people have to queue, too).

Questions to ask yourself

1 Do you currently waste customers' time by putting them on hold, or by making them wait in queues?
2 Are there ways you could make these experiences entertaining or educational?

Tips: Making the wait worthwhile

1 If you use messages for people you put on hold, make the message informative or amusing. It could include a brief testimonial from a satisfied customer, a tip that could help the caller or a thought-provoking question.
2 Change the message at least once a month, preferably once a week, especially if you have a lot of repeat callers.
3 If people have to queue in your business, consider ways to make the experience less tedious. Possibilities include having TV monitors playing amusing or instructive mini-programmes, a kiosk with free reading material, or even just a mirror (this is an old trick: when a mirror is present, people are more patient when waiting for slow-moving lifts).

Find a captive audience

The problem

Michael DiFranza wanted to find a new way to capture people's attention for advertising messages.

The strategy

While riding in the lift of his office building one day, DiFranza noticed that people never seemed to know where to look during the ride. He had the idea that, if he could find a way to offer them useful information, they wouldn't mind looking at commercial messages as well. His company, Captivate Network, Inc., places interactive flat-panel displays on lift walls. They display information about news, the weather and traffic conditions, and the bottom quarter of the screen features ten-second adverts.

The outcome

The service is already in operation in Boston, New York City and Chicago, and DiFranza has raised $50 million in investment money to expand the service to at least half a dozen additional major cities.

The lessons

As advertising spreads to more and more places, finding somewhere where it is not yet present can pay off handsomely – especially if you can sugar-coat it by also providing a useful service as DiFranza has done. Without the sweetener of useful information, people might just have found the advertising intrusive and annoying.

Questions to ask yourself

1 Is there any 'dead time' in the lives of your target population that you could use to make them aware of your business?
2 If so, how could you combine it with something that they will perceive to be of value?

Tips: Finding a captive audience

1 Consider the lifestyle of your target population. Where do they spend time? What do they do? What do they read? Is there somewhere in that range of activities where you could get their attention for long enough to make them aware of your business?
2 The range of possibilities that others have already thought of is impressive. A company called C&E New Media puts up advertising messages on toilet walls; Beach 'n' Billboard Inc. puts blanket-size impressions on the sand at public beaches; the Fruit Label Co. puts advertising stickers on the fruit and veg in supermarkets (including 15 million stickers on apples for the Ask Jeeves Internet search engine); and Key Ad LLC imprints ads on plastic hotel key cards and key-card folders.

3 Once you have thought of some possibilities, consider how you can reduce the annoyance factor by marrying your message to something useful. Consider all the things that people find helpful, such as news, maps, humour, helpful hints or tips, and inspirational quotes.

Make it fast and easy

The problem

A major bank realised that its share of automobile loans placed through dealers was inversely proportional to the length of time that customers had to wait for credit approval in the showroom. The longer it took, the more likely the customers were to say that they would make other arrangements. Their average time was 35 minutes.

The strategy

The bank came up with a way to send copies of handwritten applications quickly to each department concerned, rather than waiting for one copy of the form to make the rounds.

The outcome

The waiting time shrank to an average of five minutes. The bank's loan business doubled in eighteen months.

The lessons

The easier (which often means faster) you make it for people to deal with you, the more likely it is you will capture their business. In this age of instant gratification, no one is willing to wait for very long. Offer them a faster alternative, and they will reward you with their business.

Questions to ask yourself

1 When was the last time you took a critical look at how long it takes to perform the various functions of your business?

2   Are there elements of your service that might be combined, done in parallel or otherwise modified in order to save your customers' time?

Tips: Speeding up

1   Do a diagram in which you draw a timeline for your business. Indicate how much time typically is spent on each specific phase of serving your customer.

2   For each phase, brainstorm ways that you might speed up that function. This will work best if you put aside all preconceptions based on how it has always been done in your business or industry. If possible, involve people who are not familiar with how it is done now. Tell them the outcome that is required and let them come up with how they would achieve that result. They may come up with fresh approaches that save time.

Show them you're like them

The problem

Peter Radsliff, director of marketing for Monster Cable, realised that the company handled such a diverse group of customers that it was impossible for the Monster sales reps to make the right impression with all of the customers in their geographical area. If the rep dressed down, certain clients would take offence; if the rep dressed up, other clients would think he or she was overdressed. Either way, there would not be that quick bonding that helps establish rapport.

The strategy

Instead of giving each sales rep a geographical area to cover, Radsliff decided to use different sales reps within the same geographical area. Some call only on car stereo dealers, others only on computer stores, yet others only on audio speciality shops.

The outcome

The sales figures improved and so did the morale of the sales representatives. This way they get to know their special market extremely well, and build up closer relationships with the buyers.

The lessons

Radsliff recognised the importance of first impressions, and adjusted the system to take that into account. Influence theory has revealed that the single most important factor in whether we like someone else at first sight is whether or not we feel they are similar to us. We like people we think are similar, and we tend to be suspicious or wary of people we think are different. If you can suggest to customers that the people who represent your company are like them, you will have won half the battle.

Radsliff dared to question the way things are usually done in order to find a system that would work better. This openness leads to new opportunities, and it's useful to question the existing system periodically, even when it's working pretty well. There may be something that works better yet.

Questions to ask yourself

1 What kind of first impression does your business make on potential customers?
2 Could any part of your system be adjusted in order to improve that first impression?
3 Specifically, what can you do to give your customers the impression that your staff are like them?

Tips: Making a great first impression

1 Make a list of the ways that potential customers have their first contact with you. Include the kind of impression they get when they ring you, when they receive a letter or advertising material from you and when they see the packaging of your product.
2 Ask an outside person to give you an account of their first impressions. If you feel they might be too polite or eager to

please, have them talk to a third party about this, and let the third party report the results to you.

3 Do a simple survey of a representative sample of customers to confirm whether or not you are right in your guess about how they see your company. One way is to give them a list of positive and negative adjectives, and ask them to circle all those they think apply to your business. These could include terms such as friendly, uncaring, slow, flexible, efficient and cold. Mix up all the adjectives, and don't use more than about fifteen or else this will seem too much like work. Do, however, give them the chance to add any that are not on the list but that they feel apply to your business.

4 Brainstorm what are the important characteristics of your customers as a group. For each one, identify how that manifests itself in their appearance, in their behaviour and in their surroundings. Then consider how you might mirror some of these aspects in how your staff dress or behave, or in the appearance of your store or office.

Make sure they can see you

The problem

BigStar, an online video and DVD retailer, wanted to be sure that people were aware of them and thought of them as a 'real' company.

The strategy

They paid for the BigStar logo to be painted on several hundred trucks belonging to various businesses in Los Angeles, Dallas, San Francisco and New York. In fact, BigStar have no delivery vehicles: they use UPS parcels service to deliver their products, so these signs are only for show.

The outcome

The company report an increased consumer awareness of their existence, and are satisfied with the outcome of the campaign.

The lessons

With the plethora of dotcoms, it is increasingly difficult to get noticed, especially in a way that engenders trust. In this case, the illusion that BigStar has actual delivery vehicles gives it a down-to-earth association with good old reliable bricks and mortar.

Questions to ask yourself

1   In the minds of your customers, is your business represented in both worlds: the Internet and bricks-and-mortar? If not, might it strengthen your brand if it were?
2   How could you have this kind of representation in a low-cost way?

Tips: Getting their attention

1   If you are represented only on the Internet at this point, brainstorm how you could also have a more material presence. One possibility is to enter a partnership (see the case studies under Principle 13) with a bricks-and-mortar company.
2   If you are not represented at all on the Internet, consider how you might establish a presence there. Simply having someone build you a website is not enough: you have to find ways to get people to go to it. It may be more beneficial for you to consider how you might get a spot on a website that already exists and is already drawing eyeballs to it. One way to do this is to provide free content in exchange for a banner ad or other space on the site. For example, a restaurant might provide a weekly recipe in exchange for space on a city guide.

Make it newsworthy

Publicity is cheaper and more convincing than advertising, but if you want the press to write about your product or service you have to make it newsworthy. The product or service itself may not be news, but, as you'll see from our case studies, there's no end to the ways you can dress something up or put it into a context that makes it appealing to the press.

It's all show biz now

The problem

An innkeeper, Chuck Hilstead, wanted to come up with a way to attract more guests to his Queen Anne Inn, especially during traditionally quiet times.

The strategy

Once a year, just after Christmas, he runs a Romantic of the Year contest. The prizes include a candlelit dinner, candy, flowers and of course a night at his inn. To publicise the contest, he sends press releases to local and regional media outlets. The entrants who don't win still receive discount coupons.

The outcome

The first contest brought Hilstead thirty to forty new bookings that winter, which is traditionally the slowest time of the year for the inn. Subsequently, the contest has attracted hundreds of new customers, and has given the inn an identity as 'that place where they have the contest'.

The lessons

A contest can be an excellent way of getting attention for your business, and the prizes don't have to be huge. In this case, giving away a room for a night at a time when the inn would probably not be full anyway is not much of a sacrifice, and the other prizes are not expensive. A contest appeals to the universal desire to win something, and becomes an instant news event, especially in the local media.

It's ideal if the contest (and the prizes) are a good fit with the nature of your business. Since the Queen Anne Inn is a romantic place to stay, a Romantic of the Year contest is a natural.

Questions to ask yourself

1 What kind of contest could you run?
2 What prizes would be appropriate and affordable?
3 How could you get publicity for your contest?
4 Is there a way you could make use of the losing entries – for example, to compile a mailing list?

Tips: How to run a winning contest

1 Spend some time thinking about what kind of contest is appropriate to your business and also will be newsworthy. A humorous angle, a tie-in to a holiday or something that involves local personalities – they all add to the likelihood that the news media will give you attention. For example, a dry-cleaning establishment might offer free dry cleaning for a year to the parent who sends in a photo of the messiest teenager's room. A hotel might offer a day of pampering on Mother's Day to the woman whose child sends in

the best short essay on 'Why My Mum Deserves a Day Off'. A pet shop might offer a year's supply of dog food to the dog who wins an 'ugly contest', as judged by a local entertainer.

2 Schedule the contest so there is plenty of time for people to enter. This also means that the media can run articles about it on a slow news day.

3 Whenever possible, make sure there is some kind of visual angle. Newspapers prefer stories that have accompanying pictures. If people can post their entries, be sure to have a public event at which the prizes are awarded. Have a professional photographer take pictures in case the media don't send their own photographer to the event.

4 Try to make the losers feel like winners, too. As in our example, you might send them discount coupons or a runner-up certificate.

Be part of the show

The problem

American Jack Barringer wanted to find a way to get attention for his line of cleaning products (and, in the process, get 'filthy rich').

The strategy

He transformed himself into 'Cactus Jack', wearing a cowboy outfit and hat, and lots of jewellery. He packages his One-Shot Cleaner in the form of a yellow bullet and sells it in real ammunition boxes. He appears regularly on the QVC television home-shopping network, where his flamboyance makes him a popular guest. He also appears in his own infomercials. His unique style has made him the subject of many newspaper and magazine articles, and interviews on radio and television.

The outcome

Cactus Jack is close to his dream of becoming filthy rich. On his first appearance on QVC, he sold $100,000 worth of cleaner; on his second, he sold $200,000 worth of products in under ten minutes. In the year 2000, sales totalled over $3 million.

The lessons

In an interview with *Success* magazine, Cactus Jack said, 'I believe that the success of any brand, including mine, is 10 per cent product and 90 per cent marketing.'

Not only did he find a way to make the product look different (the bullet packaging), but made himself part of the brand. Undoubtedly, it's his entertaining style that won him his very lucrative appearances on QVC and that make his own infomercials fun to watch.

Not every entrepreneur wants to be in the public eye, and certainly not every entrepreneur wants to create a larger-than-life image, but for those with a suitable temperament it can be a fantastic marketing tool.

Questions to ask yourself

1 Is there a way to make your product or its packaging more colourful or appealing?
2 Is there any way you or another company representative could take on a higher profile in public in a way that would support your brand?

Tips: Gaining a higher profile

1 Ask yourself (and your colleagues) what kind of personality your product or service would have if it were human. Then brainstorm what kinds of ideas these terms lead to for packaging or advertising. For each idea, determine whether it's the sort of thing that would garner publicity.
2 Consider the people who work with and for you – are any of them good candidates for becoming the spokesperson for your product or company? As the marketing expert Lizz Clarke, head of LCM, says in her interview with me (see 'The Pros' View of Marketing'), this does not need to be a leader of the company: it might be a receptionist, a salesperson, even a satisfied customer. In fact, having the

spokesperson be someone other than a company leader might in itself be interesting to the media.

 ## Look for the news angle

The problem

When Viagra first came out, a chemist's named Independent DC wanted to be able to attract customers, even though the larger chains were offering the drug for less money.

The strategy

They advertised that every customer who filled a Viagra prescription there would get a free bottle of wine to add romance to the moment.

The outcome

The press, looking for new angles on the Viagra story, gave the store major coverage, which led to an increase in customers.

The lessons

Just about any product or service can be made newsworthy in one way or another. In this case, the press interest in the Viagra phenomenon was already massive, but the big problem was how to find a different angle on it, and that's what this store provided. If you can piggyback on to a topic that is already of interest to the media, it's much easier to attract their attention.

Questions to ask yourself

1 Which aspect of your business is most likely to be newsworthy?
2 Can you think of a news topic that you can use as the basis for a promotion or contest?

Tips: Making it newsworthy

1 Once a week or once a month, sit down with some colleagues and a pile of recent newspapers and news magazines.

Go through the publications and brainstorm which of the developing stories might lend themselves in some way to being linked with your business. If, for example, there has been a disaster like a flood or fire, can your business help in some way that might also be of interest to the press? In-kind donations are always more interesting than a donation of money.

2   Build up contacts with members of the press so that when you have a newsworthy item you will know who to contact. Naturally, it's easier to do this with the local press and local radio and television than the national outlets, but often reporters who start out working locally move up to national slots eventually. One way to make contact is to send the reporter a note when you see an item that he or she has done that you felt was especially good – sincere compliments are always effective.

3   If you can't afford to have a professional write your publicity material, read books or attend classes that teach you how to write effective press releases, and that tell you which are typically the slowest news days and news months (times when the media are more open to 'soft' stories that may have a promotional element).

A strange combination

The problem

David Musselwhite, a lawyer, wanted to establish an old-fashioned legal practice where clients would feel relaxed and not intimidated.

The strategy

With his wife, Musselwhite opened Legal Grounds, a combination coffee-shop and law practice (yes, this is in America – in East Dallas). One menu shows the types of espresso for sale, the other shows the fees for various legal services (an uncontested divorce is yours for $350). Consultations take place in a small office behind the kitchen, and the walls are lined with law books.

The outcome

The practice is thriving, in exactly the kind of atmosphere Musselwhite hoped to create. Although getting publicity was not his primary goal, there has been a lot of press interest, both local and national. People who read or hear about this unusual combination often show up just to make sure the place really exists, and return when they have a legal problem.

The lessons

From the standpoint of publicity, any unusual combination will be of interest to the press. In this case, the human-interest value is great as well, because this combination humanises a normally intimidating line of business. Whenever a business shows a human side, the press are likely to be fascinated.

Questions to ask yourself

1 What combinations might be possible for your business?
2 What can you do to show the human-interest side of your business, product or service?

Tips: Winning combinations

1 Start by brainstorming a list of businesses or products that you would normally think are not compatible with yours. For example, a shoe shop and a video store would not normally be considered a logical pairing.
2 For each one, consider how it could possibly combine with your business in some way. In the example of the shoe shop, what if each department sold (and showed, on monitors) videos that relate to the types of shoes being sold? In the trainers section, there could be aerobics videos; in the dress-shoe section, classic films starring Fred Astaire or Cary Grant. Stressing the human side of the transaction – that is, what we actually do when we're wearing the shoes we buy – also adds an element of warmth to the image of the store.
3 For each combination, consider whether it would be

newsworthy. In the case of the shoe shop/video sales, most likely not a lot of videos would actually be sold, but it would definitely give the local press an angle for a feature story.

Be a winner

The problem

The Lonely Planet travel guides were struggling to make money.

The strategy

This wasn't actually a strategy, more a happy development: one of the guides, the one for India, won the Thomas Cook Travel Guidebook Award.

The outcome

One of the founders, Tony Wheeler, told the *International Herald Tribune*, 'It took us to another level. It really opened doors and made a huge difference for us.' The Lonely Planet series now includes more than a hundred Travel Survival Guides to particular countries and sells well around the world.

The lessons

Getting awards can be a major factor in bringing a product or company major recognition. Some contests do not allow you to nominate yourself, but you may be able to encourage someone else to nominate you. Other contests are totally open and anyone can nominate themselves. Winning even minor awards can generate credibility and valuable press coverage.

Questions to ask yourself

1 Are you aware of the contests and awards that relate to your type of business?
2 Do you make an effort to be included in such programmes?

Tips: How to be a winner

1 Do the research: find out via trade magazines which awards

are available for your type of business and what are the deadlines and conditions of entry.

2   For contests for which you can nominate yourself, do. For others, try to find someone who is eligible to make nominations who will nominate you.

3   Whether or not you are nominated, attend awards ceremonies. They are an excellent place to network.

The business of opportunity

The problem

Max Cooper, who owns 47 McDonald's franchises in the Birmingham, Alabama, area, wanted to make sure his restaurants remained in the news.

The strategy

When he heard about record snowfalls in Michigan, he spent $4,000 to have two huge truckloads of the snow driven nearly 1,000 miles south to one of his McDonald's outlets and dumped into the children's Playland area. It gave Birmingham children the opportunity to have a white Christmas.

The outcome

The children had a great time, the parents loved it, and the stunt received massive local publicity and even some national coverage.

The lessons

Cooper has said, 'Publicity is the business of opportunity.' If you keep your ears and eyes open, there are chances almost every day for you to figure out a way to use what is happening as a means to get publicity for your business.

Questions to ask yourself

1   In terms of your publicity efforts, do you stick rigidly to a plan, or are you also looking for fresh, timely opportunities all the time?

2   What kinds of events might lend themselves to being used as the basis of publicity activities for your business?

Tips: Catching the wave

1   Take a few moments to think over the major developments of the past few months: these might include incidents of extreme weather, elections, fads and trends in toys, the openings of new businesses and so on.

2   For each one, brainstorm whether and how you could have piggybacked on to that event to get publicity for your business. Naturally, the press prefers stories that are not purely commercial. In our case study, the story was that children were getting a rare chance to enjoy the snow – a great visual story that would naturally include the details of the business that made it possible.

3   For the next six weeks, have a weekly meeting in which you and a colleague or two discuss what is happening in the news and brainstorm whether there is a good opportunity for your business to do something relevant that will give you positive publicity.

It isn't over until you say it's over

When we are children, we are taught, 'If at first you don't succeed, try, try again.' The problem is, most of us assume this means try the same thing again.

Another saying applies to this: 'If you keep on doing what you've been doing, you'll keep on getting what you've been getting.'

Therefore, if your marketing effort fails, look at how you can change either your product or service, or the way you're trying to sell it. The following case studies illustrate perseverance with a difference.

Walking (or driving) your talk

The problem

To turn a book by an unknown writer into a bestseller. The author was Wayne Dyer, the book a self-help manual called *Your Erroneous Zones*. Dyer was an unknown professor and nobody expected the book to have much of an impact. Dyer, however, decided that he would turn it into a number-one bestseller.

The strategy

Dyer bought a few hundred copies of his own book and began a six-month journey crisscrossing America. He drove from small town to small town, phoning ahead to arrange to be interviewed on the local TV and radio station and the local newspaper (in most American towns there is one of each). He also contacted the local bookshop owner (again, most small towns will have one such shop) and mentioned that he would be interviewed by the local media, so there would be demand for the book – how many copies would they be willing to take? In the course of the half-year, he drove 28,000 miles through 47 of the 50 states, having more books shipped to him as he went along. He gave over 800 interviews, and delivered almost 16,000 copies of his book to book stores.

The outcome

When Dyer was able to show the publisher how successful the book was when supported by local publicity, the publisher organised a major national advertising and publicity drive of its own. Just as Dyer had hoped, the book did become a number-one bestseller and he was able to follow it up with another hugely popular book called *Pulling Your Own Strings*. His campaign for *Your Erroneous Zones* began in 1976; he is still a popular author and lecturer.

The lessons

Probably the biggest lesson of this case study is that a big idea is nothing until it is supported by action. Dyer believed enough in his book to risk six months of his life, considerable travel expenses and the energy to give interviews day after day. This, not the nature of his book, is what sets him apart from the thousands of others who have written a book.

Questions to ask yourself

1 What could you do personally to make sure that people become aware of your product or service?
2 How much of your time and energy and other resources are you willing to put into this effort?

Tips: Going from idea to action

1 Brainstorm ways that your idea can be turned into action. Don't judge any of these ideas initially, just generate as

many of them as you can. Also, don't worry yet about how you will accomplish the idea. For example, Dyer's big idea was getting his book on the bestseller list. Initially he may have thought, If I could show the publishers that there is popular support for my book, then they would allocate money to advertising it and getting publicity for it, and that would help put it on the bestseller list.

2 Next, consider general ways that you might go about implementing the big idea. Staying with our example, maybe Dyer thought, If I could stimulate grassroots sales of my book, then the publishers would take notice.

3 Finally, brainstorm specific ways in which you could achieve your action steps. As alternatives, Dyer could have hired travelling salespeople to take the book to hundreds of bookshops across the country, or he could have posted hundreds of copies to local newspapers and radio stations, along with a press release.

4 Now evaluate each of the ideas in terms of likely impact and cost (not only in terms of money, but also in terms of your time and energy). In Dyer's case, although doing the tour himself was the most time-consuming option, he may not have been able to afford to send salespeople to do it for him, and he may have realised that merely sending out books would not be nearly as effective as being present to do interviews himself.

Where there's a will, there's a way

The problem

The author Carole Markin wanted to write a book of celebrity stories about the worst dates they ever had. The problem was that famous people have agents, managers, publicists and assistants to keep people like her from bothering her clients. Not only that, Markin was scared to talk to famous people.

The strategy

Markin started with the usual approaches: writing to the celebrities, phoning their agents and so on. A lot of the time, this didn't get her very far, so she did whatever else she could think of, including crashing parties, hanging out in front of expensive restaurants and politely approaching celebrities as they went in or came out (or even while they were eating), sneaking on to movie sets, and trying to find any kind of connections she could.

The outcome

Markin later revealed that, even after an average of two letters and ten phone calls, only 10 per cent of those she approached agreed to co-operate. However, she eventually got over a hundred celebrities, including the actress Julia Roberts and the director David Lynch, to tell her about their worst dates, and the book, called *Bad Dates*, was published.

The lessons

This case study is a great example of sheer persistence. Markin was so passionate about her goal that she overcame her own shyness, and didn't let rejections, lots of rejections, stop her. Even with a success rate of only 10 per cent, she reached her goal.

The lesson is that it's not the number of times you get rejected that matters: it's the number of times you get accepted.

Also, notice how many different approaches she used. If she'd tried only one, she would never have succeeded. Therefore, the moral is not only 'If at first you don't succeed, try, try again,' but 'If at first you don't succeed, try something different.'

Questions to ask yourself

1 Are you so passionate about your own success that you can overcome your weaknesses and fears?
2 If you need help overcoming these weaknesses and fears, where can you get it?
3 For each thing you really want to achieve, how many strategies do you have for achieving it?

4 Are you ready to ignore rejections and keep going until you succeed?

Tips: How to have the will and find the way

1 Spend a few minutes each day visualising what it would be like to have reached your goal. What will you see, what will you hear, what will you feel?
2 Read inspiring stories of people who had to persevere in order to get what they wanted. Most 'overnight successes' in any field actually had goals.
3 Always have a back-up plan and a back-up plan for the back-up plan. This is not defeatism: it's preparedness. The more possible ways you have to reach your goal, the more likely it is you will attain it.

Don't take no for an answer

The problem

The advertising agency BBDO had hoped to be chosen to represent the London radio station Kiss 100 FM, a million-pound account, but didn't make it to the shortlist.

The strategy

The ad agency made up a poster with a graphic of a large pair of lips and the legend, 'We'll put your name on everybody's lips', framed it, and sent it to the station's managing director.

The outcome

The radio station's managing director was impressed enough to add BBDO to the shortlist after all. After six days of preparation, the agency made their pitch, and won the account.

The lessons

It would have been easy for BBDO to give a philosophical shrug and accept that this time things had not gone their way. Instead, they decided not to take no for an answer and went an extra step.

They didn't argue about the decision not to include them on the shortlist: they simply made a gesture that showed they were creative and genuinely interested in being allowed to compete for the business. The best salespeople never assume that a first 'no' is final, and most of the time we shouldn't, either.

Questions to ask yourself

1 When you get a rejection, do you automatically assume that is the end of the matter even if you don't know whether a final decision has been made?
2 When you get a rejection, what might be a non-argumentative step you can take to show that you're not going to give up?
3 If it's not appropriate to go back right away, how can you keep the potential customer or client aware of you?

Tips: How not to take no for an answer

1 If the rejection is not final, consider what step you might take in order to change the other person's perception of you. It almost never works to argue – instead, the focus should be on adding value. In the case of BBDO, they were willing to invest time and creative effort to give a little sample of what they could do if they were chosen. The effort itself was probably at least as important as the product they came up with.
2 If the rejection is final, consider what steps you can take to make it more likely that the other party will come to you if they are ever dissatisfied with the choice they have made. This might entail sending them a periodic newsletter about what you've done for other customers or clients, or inviting them to a business function. Your attitude should be that of a patient suitor – not intrusive, not negative, just there and ready.

Find the way around

The problem

Nicky Southby's goal was to leave her low-paying job and buy a white Rolls-Royce to rent out for weddings. When she found a

1970 Silver Shadow for sale for $30,000, she mortgaged her house to buy it. But, when she set up her car-rental business, the local authorities confronted her with so many rules and regulations about insurance and other matters that she couldn't proceed.

The strategy

Southby set up her business as an automotive time share instead. For an annual payment of $240, each person is allowed to use the Rolls for eight hours a year.

The outcome

The time-share approach allowed her to avoid all the red tape, and to have the business she'd always wanted.

The lessons

Where there's a will, there's a way. Where ninety-nine out of a hundred people would have given up, or spent months and maybe years fighting the bureaucrats, this woman thought laterally and came up with a unique solution.

Questions to ask yourself

1 When you come up against a setback, do you accept it, do you fight it head-on, or do you think laterally to find a way around it?
2 Is there a problem confronting you at the moment, or coming up, that you can deal with by using lateral thinking?

Tips: Using lateral thinking

1 Find a comparison for your situation. In the case study, perhaps Southby thought, What else do people rent? They rent cars, but they also rent houses.
2 Then generate alternatives for the comparison. In the case of houses, people not only rent them, they also lease them, they buy them, they stay as guests and they buy time shares.
3 Finally, consider whether these alternatives lead to a solution to your problem. In the case of the examples above, time shares ended up giving Nicky the idea she needed.

The first is the hardest

The problem

The founders of the Sci-Fi Channel, Mitch Rubenstein and Laurie Silvers, devoted a year to researching whether or not it would be viable, and another year presenting the idea to the operators of U.S. cable television systems. After eighteen months, no cable operators had committed to carrying their channel.

The strategy

They kept making presentations.

The outcome

Finally, a cable operator called Telecable made a major commitment. Then, suddenly, there was a tremendous outpouring of interest, and near the time of their launch they had commitments from a hundred major cable operators. The Sci-Fi Channel is now an international success.

The lessons

Often people are very reluctant to be the first to try something new, but, as soon as at least one of their peers goes for it, they're interested, too. This means you may need to spend a disproportionate amount of time, energy and money to woo your first major client or customer, especially when what you are offering is something new.

Questions to ask yourself

1   If you're discouraged by a lack of progress, might you be just on the point of breaking through?
2   Have you allocated enough resources to get yourself past the point of landing the first important customer?
3   When you win that first crucial customer or client, are you ready to let the others know about it?

Tips: Winning the first customer

1 Consider offering a major discount to the first one or two major customers. In some cases, it may even be worth offering your product or service free.

2 Offer the first one or two major customers or clients an iron-clad guarantee that makes them feel totally secure in trying out your product or service.

3 Piggyback the new product or service on to another one that they want. If you don't have one, make an arrangement with someone who does (but who is not a competitor, obviously) to let yours be a value-added combination with theirs.

Never give up

The problem

A Dallas housewife, Nancy Strong, teamed up with a partner to open a travel agency. The partner promised a $200,000 account to get them started, but couldn't deliver and dropped out.

The strategy

Strong could have given up, too, but instead she started doing cold calls on potential customers.

The outcome

Six weeks later, Strong found her first big customer. That was enough to launch the business and to keep her going. Thirteen years later she had achieved $20 million in billings, and sold the firm.

The lessons

Strong decided to keep going even though she encountered a massive setback even before the business was established. This kind of perseverance requires faith and courage. Strong also realised that if you don't ask you don't get. She started knocking on doors and asking for business and didn't stop until she landed her first big account. Many people are afraid to ask for what they really want.

Questions to ask yourself

1 Do you have sufficient faith in yourself and your business to keep going if you encounter a major setback?
2 Are you prepared to ask for business until you get it?
3 Are you prepared to do cold calling if necessary?

Tips: Staying the course

1 First, be aware that almost every business does go through difficult times, especially in its first few years. To some extent you can anticipate obstacles, but there will always be surprises. The awareness that this is the rule rather than the exception can in itself help.
2 If you undergo a difficult period, avoid the temptation to go into a state of denial. Decide immediately what action needs to be taken, and throw yourself into it. The biggest source of stress is feeling out of control, and, when you act, you begin to feel more in control immediately, even if your actions don't pay off right away.
3 Don't be afraid to ask. In our example, Strong asked for orders, but you may also at some point need to ask for financial help or emotional support. You may need to ask employees to continue working during a time when you cannot afford to pay them their full salaries. If you show confidence in yourself, so will the people you ask for help.

Outwait them

The problem

When Jennifer Gilbert started an events-planning company, she relied on cold calling to get appointments with potential clients. However, most of them, including a bank she wanted as a client, never returned her calls.

The strategy

Feeling totally frustrated, Gilbert went to one of the banks in person, carrying fifty yellow balloons, and waited in the lobby for five hours before anyone would see her. But when they finally did, they took one look at her, laughed at her nerve and determination, and listened to her sales pitch.

The outcome

The bank became a major client. She started the company in 1994 with $50, and in a recent year her revenues were $15 million.

The lessons

It took courage for Gilbert to go to the bank in person, and she admitted that she sat in the lobby with a sinking heart, but ultimately it paid off. Sheer determination and the willingness to take action often win the day.

Questions to ask yourself

1   Would you have had the courage to do what Gilbert did? Would it help your business if you did?
2   Do you take rejection personally?
3   Do you have sufficient determination to get past the obstacles you are bound to encounter in growing your business?

Tips: Hanging in there

1   Mentally go over the times in the recent past when you took 'no' for a final answer. Consider whether it would make sense to revisit any of those potential customers with a different approach.
2   Brainstorm how you impress potential customers who initially say no. Once again, it's a matter of being ready to do something different. In our example, Gilbert didn't continue to ring the bank because she realised that wasn't working. Therefore, she decided to do something else – to confront them on their own turf.

3 Brainstorm how you can make your perseverance good-natured, rather than annoying. In Gilbert's case, the fifty yellow balloons not only represented her business, but they also gave a humorous aspect to her vigil.

Consider the opposite

One of our problems is that when we know a lot about our business, we get stuck into the box of how things are usually done. It's difficult to get out of this mindset and approach a problem in a fresh way, yet that's exactly what we need to do. In Buddhism, they call this 'beginner's mind' – that is, the open state of mind of someone who doesn't yet know what can't be done; and so, often, does it.

A good way to get out of this box is to think about how everybody else does whatever you want to do, and then consider doing the opposite. Sometimes the opposite is not practical but leads you to something that is. The following case studies will show you how this approach has worked for many people – including one of the most famous tycoons of the Industrial Revolution.

Variations on your theme

The problem

Collecting a debt.

The strategy

In his excellent book *What a Great Idea!!* Chic Thompson tells the story of what he did when he was owed a considerable amount of money and discovered that his debtor was about to move out of town. He decided to try doing something different:

Everybody else would send a formal invoice; Thompson sent a cartoon of himself lying on the floor with a knife coming out of his back, and the caption, 'I trusted you'.

Everybody else would send the invoice to the man's office; Thompson sent it to the man's home.

Everybody else would send a letter-sized invoice; Thompson sent his in a hand-addressed three-foot package.

Everybody else uses the postal service; Thompson sent his with a next-day-delivery service.

The outcome

The man paid up. Not only that, Thompson printed up several versions of his collection of cartoons and sold them in office-supply stores. Articles were written about them in newspapers in the United States, Europe and even Pakistan.

The lessons

This is a great example of when our general principle, 'do something different', is really important. It's probably a safe bet to guess that Thompson was not the only person to whom the man in question owed money. Had Thompson merely sent a normal invoice, it might have been lost in the shuffle. Instead, he made his demand for repayment stand out in every way. Since it was delivered to the man's home, perhaps his wife or another family member opened it, and asked him why he was not paying this debt. Therefore, the lesson is: when you fear that doing the usual thing will not get results, do the unusual.

Questions to ask yourself

1. What are the usual ways of doing things in your line of business?
2. What alternatives to these usual ways can you come up with?
3. Might there be a way that you can market or otherwise take additional advantage of innovations you come up with for handling your business problems?

Tips: How to make your efforts stand out

1 Make it a different size. This could apply to many things: instead of a normal-size business card, use one that unfolds to a much larger size; instead of packaging your product in a small box, package it in a large box and use that as a selling point (for example, 'the little stain remover that takes care of BIG stains'); instead of sending people a letter, send them a rolled-up poster.

2 Try variations on the delivery system. If your competitors use people to hand out leaflets, how about using people dressed up as cartoon characters to hand out yours? If your competitors are sending direct mail using printed address labels, how about using home workers to hand-address yours? If your competitors are using billboards, try using lots of small stickers.

3 Use a different medium. If everybody else is using print ads, might it be more effective to use radio ads? If everybody else sends a letter, might it be more powerful to send a photo-story? Or, if your message is brief (such as a website address you'd like people to check out), how about putting it inside fortune cookies you hand out during the lunch hour?

4 If you find a particularly effective way to get your message across, consider whether it might be something that you can market, perhaps to people in the same situation who are not directly competitive with you. For example, an estate agent who comes up with a piece of software that is effective at showing potential buyers property via email might be able to market it to estate agents all around the country.

From weakness to strength

The problem

In 1926, Ward Cosgrove, an American who was working for a canning company, came across a different kind of pea in Europe: the Prince of Wales garden pea. He was interested in marketing it in the United States, but the problem was how to make the large, oval, wrinkly pea appeal to consumers who were used to smooth, small, round peas.

The strategy

Cosgrove decided to turn a weakness into a strength. He later recalled, 'We made it a marketing feature by calling the brand "Green Giant".' The advertising implied that bigger is better, and, a few years later, the advertising genius Leo Burnett invented a character for the packaging and for ads, the Jolly Green Giant (who had a distinctive 'Ho ho ho!' laugh).

The outcome

The campaigns were so successful that by the 1940s the Prince of Wales peas totally dominated the market.

The lessons

What may initially be shortcomings can be transformed into a strength. A ketchup manufacturer did the same thing more recently, by suggesting that the fact that its ketchup pours more slowly than the competition's is a sign of quality.

Questions to ask yourself

1   What are the main drawbacks of your product or service?
2   How could these drawbacks be seen as strengths or advantages?
3   How can you help your customers to see these aspects of your business in the new light?

Tips: Turning weaknesses into strengths

1   Think about the possible positive connotations of the potentially negative features. For example, if you take more time to do a job than your competition, that could also be a sign that you take more care over it. Or, if your product costs more, that could be a sign that it is of higher quality.
2   Consider ways to underline the positive interpretation with a symbol or slogan (just as the food company used the Jolly

Green Giant). For example, you might use a slogan like 'It takes us a little longer because we do it right.' A good example is what Hallmark did when they found the greeting-card market flooded with cheaper cards: they came up with the slogan 'When you care enough to send the very best.' The implication was that people who sent cheaper cards didn't care as much about the recipients as people who spent a bit more for Hallmark cards.

Put it into reverse

The problem

Henry Ford wanted to find a quicker way of assembling cars. The system at that point brought the workers to the parts and materials.

The strategy

Ford considered the reverse of the 'obvious' way of assembling cars. Instead of asking how they could get the workers to the parts, he asked how they could get the parts to the workers. The result was the assembly line.

The outcome

It became possible to turn out cars at a much faster rate and therefore to bring the price down. This discovery was a significant development in the birth of the massive automobile industry, and made Ford the dominant player for many years.

The lessons

Periodically it's worth asking whether the way we do things is the best way. Ironically, Japanese car manufacturers were able to take the lead sixty or seventy years later partly because Ford's way had by then become the obvious way and was not being questioned. As well as questioning the assumption that people would buy only large cars, they questioned whether the assembly line was still the most efficient way to build cars. They found that forming workers into teams and giving them variety in their tasks made them happier and more productive.

Reversing assumptions is an excellent creativity technique for all kinds of goals.

Questions to ask yourself

1 What are your assumptions about the goal you have?
2 What new ideas come to mind when you try reversing those assumptions?

Tips: Getting a fresh view of what you do

1 Make a list of the major aspects of your business. For example, 'We send out catalogues showing our line of office furniture', 'We target small- to medium-sized companies that are upgrading their office furniture', and so on.
2 For each aspect, write down what would be the opposite: 'We do not send out catalogues', 'We do not target small- to medium-sized companies that are upgrading their office furniture'.
3 For each opposite, brainstorm what might be a practical interpretation of the reversal. For example, if we don't send out catalogues, what do we do instead? Maybe we send out fliers and charge people a pound to receive the catalogue – might that weed out the people who aren't really in the market anyway? If we don't target small- to medium-sized companies, who do we target? Maybe we target buyers of home-office flats. Maybe we target multinational firms that are setting up new offices in this country. Generate as many ideas as possible.
4 Only when you've generated lots of ideas, go through them to find those worth further consideration.

Use golden oldies

The problem

When the B&Q Superstore opened in Macclesfield, they wanted to find a workforce that would be reliable, courteous and hardworking.

The strategy

Management asked themselves what kind of employees would be likely to be motivated to work, to have experience to draw upon and to evoke positive feelings from customers. They came up with the answer: older people, many of whom like to work part-time. Having a job gives them extra income and, equally important for many of them, a sense of purpose and a place to be with other people. The branch decided to hire only employees over the age of 49.

The outcome

This branch has brought in more revenue than the company average, absenteeism is lower than average, profits are higher, customer satisfaction is higher, and theft is lower.

The lessons

Hiring older workers is the opposite of the emphasis on youth in our culture, so the managers did really do something different. If hiring older workers is not appropriate for your business, there may be another group that is typically overlooked but that might give you an edge. These might be women returning to work after having had a child, or people with physical disabilities, for example.

Another example is Chasma, Inc., a games development company that employs teenagers. The company's CEO is himself only eighteen, and he told reporters, 'A lot of kids have skills, but no one will give them a chance. We're giving them a chance to make a difference.'

Questions to ask yourself

1 If you will be hiring additional people, what qualities will you be looking for?
2 What kinds of people are most likely to have the qualities you're looking for?
3 Have you considered a variety of types of workers – for instance, older workers, students, people who could work from their homes, workers with disabilities – and asked

yourself whether you might gain by going against the hiring trends?

Tips: Finding the right people

1 Consider groups that are often overlooked: those who are younger, those who are older, those who are returning to work after having children or taking time off for other reasons, and those who are able to work only part-time. In many cases, they will have excellent motivation to get and keep a job because they know how difficult it can be to get one.

2 Go beyond the usual want ads, and put up notices in places where the kinds of people you're looking for may be found. This could include student centres, libraries and shopping malls.

3 Offer incentives that would appeal to the kind of person you're looking for. For example, older workers might welcome the chance to work part-time, and workers with families might appreciate the opportunity to do some of their work at home.

Be colourful

The problem

Ed Nye, a beverage distributor, wanted to increase his company's share in a highly competitive field.

The strategy

At a time when everybody else was offering clear, colourless soft drinks, Nye decided to offer brightly coloured ones. He also decided to use equally bright ads. One showed lightning striking a drink called Electric Blue Raspberry. Another showed a neon banana, introducing a drink called Ba-Neon-A.

The outcome

Nye said that people either loved or hated the ads (and the bright drinks). A lot of people must have loved them, because in the course of three years sales tripled, and the customers who signed on included major companies such as the restaurant chain Chi Chi's, and the Princess and Carnival cruise lines.

The lessons

Nye applied what in the financial markets often is called 'contrarian thinking' – another way of saying, 'When everybody's doing something, do the opposite.' When others were pushing clear drinks, Nye opted to go to the other extreme.

When you have an unusual product, the way you market it should match the product. In this case, when the drinks were colourful, the ads had to be equally colourful to get the point across.

Questions to ask yourself

1 Are you trying to ride the tide along with everyone else, or is there a way you could succeed by going against the tide?
2 Are the ways that you are advertising or marketing your product or service in line with the nature of the product or service itself?

Tips: Trying the contrarian approach

1 First, make up a list of ten things that all of your competitors and/or their products or services have in common. This might include common elements of product features, packaging, how they're advertised or promoted, and so on.
2 For each of the ten, jot down what would be the opposite or at least very different. For example, if you make shampoo and all of your competitors sell their shampoo in bottles, you might write down options such as selling yours in a tin. Or, if you're a personal success coach and all your competitors give consultations via the phone, consider giving consultations in person at lunch, or while your clients work out at a health club.
3 Going down the list of alternatives, identify the ones that are both practical and likely to make you and your product or

service noticed, and choose the ones to implement on a trial basis to assess the response.

 ## Be happy

The problem

Michelle Lubow, head of Design One, found that her independent sales reps were bringing in too many low-margin orders. This gave them a good commission, but didn't help the company's profits.

The strategy

Lubow fired the sales reps and decided to run the entire business by herself.

The outcome

Sales dropped, she lost several accounts, and she's not finding new customers as rapidly as when the reps were out in the field. This may sound like an outcome that doesn't belong in a book of success stories, but there are two mitigating factors. First, the accounts she still has are for high-margin sales, and have grown in size. Second, Lubow is much happier running the business as a one-person operation. She told *Inc.* magazine, 'I was spending all day helping the sales staff, and I was no longer enjoying running the business.'

The lessons

The bottom line isn't always the bottom line. Work has to bring personal satisfaction as well as money, and in this case Lubow sacrificed a bit of the latter to have a lot of the former. As businesses grow, their very success can lead to conditions that make them less satisfying for their founders.

Questions to ask yourself

1 Are you enjoying your business?
2 Are there changes that you could make that would allow you to enjoy your business more?

3 Have you evaluated the price of these changes and evaluated whether or not they are worth making?

Tips: Enjoying your business

1 Remember why you got into the business you are in. What were your hopes and dreams for it? Which of your values related to going into this business?
2 Consider whether these hopes and dreams have been realised, or are on the way to being realised. Also consider whether your business, as it is now, still links to the values most important to you.
3 If there is a discrepancy between what you hoped to gain from the business and what you are actually gaining from it (emotionally as well as financially), consider what changes could bring this back into balance.

Get them before someone else does

The problem

Unilever wanted to have a presence in underdeveloped markets.

The strategy

They started what they call the Everyman Project. It began in India in 1994, where the company supplied its laundry soap for women doing the wash in the Ganges. Next it went to Brazil, where in the poorest areas the company sells a special shampoo for wavy, mulatto hair. Additional locales are Africa and Latin America. All of these products are sold very cheaply to make them affordable to the target population.

The outcome

Unilever is building a presence in markets being ignored by most other international companies. Although the revenue is just enough to make the programme pay for itself, by doing the opposite of everyone else – that is, going into a market that seems unprofitable – it is building brand loyalty in markets that will mature over time.

The lessons

When considering a market segment, it pays to think of the future as well as the present. Banks have been doing this for years, encouraging youngsters to open accounts that are, in strict financial terms, more trouble than they are worth. The assumption is that the child will stay with the same bank when he or she grows up.

Questions to ask yourself

1 Are there any 'unripe' market segments that you might cultivate now because they hold promise for the future?
2 How could you deal with such segments now in a way that will capture their loyalty?

Tips: Finding customers early

1 Make a list of all the types of people who currently do *not* use your product or business. By each, jot down why they don't – this may be because they're too young, they don't have enough money, the product is not aimed at them and so forth.
2 Review the list and see whether any of these groups are likely to be customers sometime in the future if and when their circumstances change – that is, when they are older, or when they are earning more money.
3 Brainstorm how you might capture some of these customer groups now. What would you have to do to make your business relevant to them? It might require you to have a separate, lower-cost version of your product or service, or to modify it.

Sell even to your enemies

The problem

IBM wanted to maximise the returns from its huge expenses for research and development (estimated to be $5 billion).

The strategy

IBM decided to license its patented technology and sell elements of
its core systems to anyone – including rivals.

The outcome

IBM made deals with companies including Apple, Hitachi and
Canon for IBM components that go into products directly
competitive with the ones made by IBM. Just one deal, for Hitachi
to buy IBM chips, was expected to bring in $100 million. In two
years, technology sales revenue went from $600 million to $1
billion.

The lessons

Although it's counterintuitive, sometimes co-operating with competitors not only improves your bottom line, it can open up the
marketplace further as well. Furthermore, the use of IBM technology by other leading computer manufacturers is good for IBM's
image. The notion that one must never do anything that helps a
competitor is dead – as long as you help yourself in the process,
too.

Questions to ask yourself

1 Do you have assets (knowledge, patents, anything that could
   be licensed) that you could use to help bring in more revenue?
2 How could you sell these assets, even to competitors, in a
   way that would be beneficial to you and to them?

Tips: Sell it and keep it

1 Make a list of all the assets associated with your business. Be
   sure to consider all aspects, including any original software,
   business procedures, databases and so forth.
2 Go over the list and consider which ones would be of value
   to others, and how you could sell or license them, or otherwise mine them for additional value. This could even

include writing a book or manual for a commercial publisher.

3   For the most promising ones, evaluate both the positive and
possible negative impact of sharing them.

Learn from the competition – and everybody else

To stay competitive these days, you have to keep learning all the time. Study what your successful competitors are doing. Study what successful businesses in totally different fields are doing, and how you might apply that to your business. Study the trends, the new software and hardware that might make your business more successful. Make your skill part of what you are selling. Obviously you can't do everything yourself, but it's important to know enough to be able to outsource the parts that you can't handle yourself.

The marketing side of this comes in letting your customers or clients know that you (and/or your company) are on the cutting edge of new developments, and that they will get the most up-to-date products or service when they deal with you.

 Back to school

The problem

David Liniger, founder and head of the RE/MAX real-estate company, wanted to get the information required in order to establish and maintain a successful real-estate franchise company.

The strategy

Liniger decided to dedicate a substantial amount of time and money to ongoing training and development. He told *Success* magazine, 'Even when we were absolutely broke, we went to every seminar we could.' These included seminars on financial statements, public speaking, collections, business planning, time management, and sales negotiations. 'We'd act like sponges,' he says, 'taking copious notes, and then afterward we'd sit down together and ask how this applies to our company, how can we use this principle?'

The outcome

RE/MAX became a successful real-estate franchise company.

The lessons

Especially these days, when almost every type of business and industry is changing faster than ever before, constant education and retraining is necessary. As Liniger points out, this should be a number-one priority, even when money is short. Also, it's important to look at information in the light of its specific application to the task at hand. Many people go to workshops but never carefully consider exactly and specifically how they will apply the new information they have gained.

Questions to ask yourself

1 Have you made a commitment to educate yourself (and your staff) fully in all the fields that relate to what you do? Are you willing to spend the investment of time and money this requires?

2 When you go to workshops and seminars, and read trade publications, do you take time to consider exactly how you can apply the new information to your business?

Tips: Staying on top of your field

1 When you or someone else from your company attends a workshop or other training event, set aside time for that person to share their new information with the others in your business who could benefit from it.

2 If you can't find workshops that address your needs, hire a specialist to come in and teach one for your company. If

     possible, spread the cost by joining with non-competitors who may also be interested in sending people to attend the workshop.

3 Assign each staff member to monitor one publication relevant to your business and to do a monthly presentation of vital information they have gleaned from it.

Ask the experts

The problem

Elizabeth McLaughlin's company, the Hot Topic, sells trendy club wear to American teens and needs to have its finger on the pulse of quickly changing fashions.

The strategy

It sends scouts to rock concerts to keep tabs on any emerging styles, responds quickly by using domestic suppliers and keeps its order cycle under sixty days.

The outcome

Last year, the company posted sales of $240 million, up 42 per cent from the previous year.

The lessons

The best source of information about customers is … customers. If you can go where your customers are and observe their behaviour, you can stay ahead of the curve. Especially in areas like fashion, which change even more quickly than most other fields, being nimble is of the essence.

Questions to ask yourself

1 Are you keeping enough of an eye on what your customers do (as well, perhaps, as what they say in surveys or on questionnaires) to keep track of likely changes in what they want?

2 Have you maximised your ability to respond quickly when customer preferences change?

3   Is there anything you could learn from fields such as fashion, which have developed techniques for responding quickly to changes in customer behaviour?

Tips: Staying ahead of the curve

1   Hire 'spies' who spend time with your customers in their natural habitat and report back to you on a regular basis.
2   Make a special effort to identify and track the preferences of the early adopters in your customer base – those who either set the trends or are the first to spot and follow them. You might even give such customers special privileges or status in order to get their feedback.
3   Find the journalists or columnists who cover your type of business who tend to be on the leading edge of developments. Pay attention to the implications their predictions and analyses might have for your business.

Get them while they're young

The problem

International perfume companies such as Guerlain, Bulgari, Versace and Givenchy wanted to find a new segment for their businesses.

The strategy

They developed perfumes aimed at young customers – very young. Perfumes such as Royal Heirs and Petits et Mamans are designed for youngsters from birth through the early teens. The packaging includes cartoons and sometimes games are enclosed. One company was so successful with children's perfumes that it also developed a line of toiletries for children. Generally, the fragrances are light and based on fruits and flowers.

The outcome

Although these perfumes represent only one to two per cent of the overall prestige-perfume market, it's a very fast-growing segment.

In France, the gain has been 40 per cent over the last 2 ye
with the perfumes costing anything up to £30, the profit n
considerable.

The lessons

Whether or not one thinks that expensive perfumes for kids
positive development, it's true that in general these days pro
that used to be considered for adults only have spawned offsh
for youngsters. Not only does this create a new market, but it
offers a way to capture loyal customers while they're young.

Questions to ask yourself

1 In your line of business, is there a way to adapt your produ
   or service to appeal to children (or their parents, on th
   child's behalf)?
2 If you create a kids' offshoot, how can you best use it as a
   direct path to the products or services you provide to adults?
3 Even if you can't come up with a product or service designed
   for children directly, can you create something for them that
   may help you to capture their parents' business? (For example, an accounting firm might commission and distribute a
   children's book about earning and saving money.)

Tips: Appealing to the child

1 Stay current on what kids are up to these days – what they
   find entertaining, what their aspirations are. If you don't
   have children yourself, make the effort to get to know the
   children of friends and ask them lots of questions. Consider
   how this information may relate to your business.
2 If it doesn't make sense for your business to appeal to children, consider that there may be a way for it to appeal to the
   adult's 'inner child'. There's no question that a new sense of
   playfulness is appearing in the design of many products for
   adults (for example, the Swatch Smart Car and the iMac).
3 Consider other niches that are age-related. Perhaps there are
   ways your business could appeal to older customers, or to
   people in the midlife-crisis phase.

Let the figures speak

The problem

In 1998, the Vermont Teddy Bear Company was making serious losses and was desperate to turn the business around.

The strategy

The new CEO, Elisabeth Robert, noticed that about 70 per cent of the bears sold at their Manhattan outlet were shipped as gifts. Realising that the company was in the gift business rather than the teddy bear business, she closed down the retail stores and put the focus on marketing the bears as gifts that can be sent on special occasions just the way flowers are.

The outcome

In 1999, the company earned nearly $2 million on a turnover of about $22 million, and, in the first six months of 2000, profits were up over 100 per cent.

The lessons

It's surprisingly easy to be mistaken about the business you really are in, but the clues as to how the business can be focused more effectively are likely to be hidden in the data you already have. It pays to examine the data and look for patterns you may not have noticed previously.

Questions to ask yourself

1 Is it possible that rethinking the business you are in might lead you to greater profits?
2 Have you examined all the data available to you in order to learn as much as possible about the strong and weak points of your business?

Tips: Finding what business you are in

1 Analyse your sales figures by various categories. You may find that Pareto's Principle, also known as the 80-20 Rule,

applies to your business. It states that generally 80 per cent of the profits are generated by 20 per cent of the customers, or 20 per cent of the product line. When you are able to 'fire' the 80 per cent of the customers who don't add to the bottom line, or to eliminate the products that are not profitable, you streamline your operation and increase profitability.

2   Describe your business in terms of the benefits your customers get from your product or service. That may help you come up with ideas for which aspects could be emphasised further to increase the business's appeal. The most often cited example of this is McDonald's, which realised early on that it was selling speed and convenience rather than food.

3   Ask your customers what they like best about your business and what they like least. The natural tendency would be to spend most of your energy on fixing the things they dislike, but it may make more sense to put the resources into boosting the things they like best. For example, the owner of a restaurant might find out that his or her customers really like the exotic ambience, but dislike the high prices. Rather than cut the prices, it may make more sense to make the dining experience even more exotic and entertaining, to the point where customers feel the high prices are worth it.

Tuning in to teens

The problem

The ad agency North Castle Partners wanted to find out first-hand what teens are thinking and buying, in order to be able to develop effective ads targeting the teen market.

The strategy

The agency made a deal with four schools: executives from the agency teach biweekly advertising and marketing classes, and in exchange they are allowed to operate focus groups with the students. The activities have included drawing storyboards for products, assembling time capsules that epitomise their lives and playing various games related to products. The agency also invites the students to visit the company headquarters, where the youngsters produce their own radio adverts.

The outcome

The agency is able to gather information weekly, which, it feels, has given it an advantage over companies that rely on data that may be out of date by the time it is assembled into more traditional marketing reports. Because the executives see the same students throughout the term, they are able to establish a deeper relationship, which, they say, leads to information with greater depth. The agency has been able to secure major clients whose products have teen appeal, including Coca-Cola and Nabisco.

The lessons

If you want to get something from people, you also have to give them something. Although some have questioned whether the kind of commercial venture mentioned in our case study belongs in schools, the participating schools feel that the classes offered by the advertising executives have been extremely valuable to the participating students. If you can tap directly into the teen market, or any other segment of the market, you can mine it for valuable information.

Questions to ask yourself

1　Would it help your business to get more information – and more *in-depth* information – about your customer target group?
2　Are there institutions that might help you access members of your target group?
3　What can you offer the institutions and/or the customers in exchange for the time and energy they will give you in focus groups or other research activities?

Tips: Getting closer to the target group

1　If appropriate, offer to teach classes or workshops in your speciality, in exchange for access to members of the target group. This need not be limited to schools: other possible sites include recreation centres and groups of hobbyists. Obviously, if children are involved, parental permission will be necessary.

2 It may be possible to involve a charity in your research work, in exchange for a donation. The members of the target group may be more inclined to participate if they know a charity will benefit.

3 You may be able to piggyback a research session with an activity the members of the target group would enjoy. For example, you could screen a film and the price of admission could be participation in a focus group.

Learn from the competition

The problem

The Ford Company had an accounts-receivable department of 500 people and hoped to cut down to 400 people.

The strategy

They installed a new computer system so some of the tasks could be automated. But, in the course of researching the problem, they heard that Mazda employed only five people in their accounts-receivable department. Spurred by this information, Ford rethought the problem and discovered that their system required far too many checks, verifications and cross-checks. They were able to go from fourteen steps to only three.

The outcome

Ford improved the efficiency of their accounts-receivable department by more than 400 per cent.

The lessons

The first lesson is to keep an eye on what the competition is doing. There's no need for everyone to reinvent the wheel, or to assume that, just because the competition is doing it, it must be wrong. Why not learn from the others doing what you're doing?

Second, often we think too small. We consider how we could make savings or increases in efficiency of 5 or 10 per cent, when in fact major improvements could be possible if we were willing to rethink radically what we are doing. Often the block is that we are so used to the way things have always been done that we can't even conceive of a different way of doing them.

Finally, it's important to make sure we're asking the right question. Ford reformulated the question, from 'How can fewer people do the same amount of work (with the help of computers)?' to 'How can we cut down the amount of work to be done?'

Questions to ask yourself

1 Are you aware enough of what your competitors are doing?
2 Are you looking at all aspects of the problem, or are you assuming there's only one way to approach it?

Tips: Thinking outside the box

1 Check how the competition are handling the same kinds of situations. They may have achieved a breakthrough you can emulate. This doesn't require industrial espionage: in many cases it's just a matter of having a friend or colleague deal with the competing business and pay attention. It can also be useful to read the company's annual report and all its brochures and advertising material.
2 Check how businesses that are not competitors but that have some similar functions handle them. For example, a florist looking for more efficient ways of delivering flowers could study businesses that deliver any kinds of goods.
3 Bring in outsiders who are not familiar with the way things are done and get them to brainstorm possible approaches.

Big money from small ideas

The problem

RSI Insurance, of Peoria, Illinois, wanted to encourage their employees to come up with suggestions for how the company could save money.

The strategy

RSI invites employees to submit their ideas using the company's computer network. For each idea, used or not, the employee gets a $2 bill. If an employee's idea is used, he or she becomes eligible for a quarterly drawing for cash prizes between $50 and $100. Those whose ideas save the company at least $5,000 a year, or who submit five or more usable ideas, join the 'all-star' team, which is honoured at quarterly company-wide gatherings.

The outcome

Lots of savings have been made. One employee came up with an idea that saved the company almost $150,000 in one year. Another made 49 usable suggestions in under a year. Morale is good and lots of suggestions continue to pour in.

The lessons

If you give people an incentive, they will help you achieve what you want. Notice that in this case the rewards are rather modest, financially speaking. The company found that offering big rewards actually was counterproductive – it kept people from submitting little ideas with benefits that can really add up. Notice also that not all rewards cost money – honouring the most effective and prolific participants at quarterly meetings is free, but highly effective.

Questions to ask yourself

1 Are you getting suggestions for achieving what you want from the people who work for or with you?
2 If not, how can you motivate those people to make good suggestions?
3 How can you keep the incentives small enough to be affordable but big enough to feel worthwhile to the participants?
4 What rewards are available other than money?

Tips: Getting good suggestions

1 Make it easy for people to make suggestions. A dusty suggestion box tucked away in some corner is not inviting. One

idea is to use a large Perspex box, so people can see that lots of suggestions are coming in. If necessary, prime the pump by putting in a few of your own.

2 Give people quick feedback on their ideas. Some businesses review suggestions only quarterly or monthly. That's too slow – rewarding people is more effective when it's done promptly.

3 Use incentives that people really want. Don't assume they'll be thrilled with a coffee mug or T-shirt with the company logo. Ask them what they'd like, or offer them a menu of options. Choices might include cinema tickets, free meals at a local restaurant, magazine subscriptions and boxes of chocolates.

4 When a suggestion saves a lot of money, the reward should be larger, but some of it can come in the form of recognition. Being publicly thanked and given a certificate may mean more to some employees than the cash prize.

Getting a response

The problem

The response rate to marketing surveys is normally quite low, which makes the results unreliable. How can the response rate be raised?

The strategy

A marketing research firm designed the OPUS, a sleek, elegant-looking box that is posted to the potential respondent. It is accompanied by a letter and a five-dollar bill as an advance thank-you for responding. Inside the box are a hundred cards that describe a situation, and four compartments into which the cards can be sorted: agree; partly agree; disagree; and no opinion. For instance, one company used this system to find out what aspects of painting and decorating were particularly troublesome for DIY types.

The outcome

In over two hundred surveys of the European markets, using the OPUS method yielded an average response rate of over 92 per cent. Using information gleaned from an OPUS survey, one client captured about 40 per cent of the consumer paint market in a few months.

The lessons

The reason most people aren't interested in filling in survey forms is that it takes time, it's not much fun and there's nothing in it for them. The OPUS, by contrast, gives people an immediate incentive (the $5 bill). Most people feel obligated to respond once they take the money. Also, the box is impressive, which helps the respondent to feel important, and the actual process is physical and fast. Whereas answering a list of questions may remind people of school work, using the OPUS is more like a game.

Questions to ask yourself

1 Are you using any techniques to get vital input from your target population? If so, are you being successful?
2 If not, how can you make the survey process more enjoyable for the respondents?
3 Is there any other aspect of your business that might benefit from being made more fun or rewarding for the customer?

Tips: Getting customers to respond to surveys

1 Give people an incentive to respond. This may be less expensive than having to conduct a much larger survey in order to get an adequate number of responses. The incentive does not have to be cash, of course. Other possibilities include a discount coupon, a free ticket to some event or entry into a prize draw.
2 Make it fun for them to respond by using an unusual format for the survey, perhaps including cartoons, or a format that reminds them of a quiz show, or anything else that makes the process gamelike.

3 Try out a variety of different formats for your survey on small groups, and then use the most effective one for your larger mailing.

Count chickens before they're hatched

The problem

Frank Perdue wanted to introduce his Perdue Farms chicken to New York City in the early seventies, but he wanted to be sure to go about it the right way.

The strategy

Perdue first spent six months there talking to every butcher he could find. His son, James Perdue, told *Forbes* magazine, 'He took notes on yellow pads and amassed 20 of them – 800 pages. Just before he left New York, he was in a phone booth at La Guardia Airport and left one of his yellow pads there. When he later found out that it was probably picked up as garbage and taken to a land-fill, he tracked down the landfill and got it back.'

The outcome

New York City became an important market for Perdue Farms.

The lessons

Even though Perdue had already had success in other markets, he recognised that New York City was different from them. Rather than assuming he knew what this market would want, he did research. He went directly to the people who would know most about the eating habits of New Yorkers, butchers, and he did it himself rather than asking a third party to do it. Listening is almost always a good idea.

Questions to ask yourself

1 If you are considering expanding into a different market, have you considered the possibility that it is different from the ones in which you already operate?

2　What is the most direct way you could find out the needs and preferences of the people in the new market? Who are the experts?

3　How can you do at least some of this research yourself, in order to get a first-hand impression of the situation?

Tips: Getting to know the marketplace

1　First, identify who knows the target group of customers best.

2　Pick the brains of these experts. Often this is as simple as just asking, as Perdue did.

3　Do at least part of the research yourself, preferably at the beginning. Third parties may miss important information, especially if they are following a format such as a list of survey questions.

No man (or woman or business) is an island

One of the rules of the new economy is finding partners. Symbiosis is the goal, and sometimes companies even find ways of co-operating with their competitors in ways that help both. Even if you don't go that far, it's highly likely that there are businesses with which you could collaborate to the benefit of both. Similarly, your employees or customers can be your partners in your endeavours.

The key: making it worthwhile for people to do what you'd like them to do. The following case studies illustrate the benefits of this kind of co-operation.

Riding piggyback

The problem

How to cash in on the Beanie Baby craze.

The strategy

A husband-and-wife team, Sue and Leslie Fox, noticed that there was no buying guide to the collectable Beanie Babies collection. They approached publishers, but found no interest. So they dipped into their young daughter's college fund and invested $100,000 in publishing the guide themselves. *The Beanie Baby Handbook* calls itself an investment guide to Beanie Baby toys, and estimates what each Baby might be worth by 2008. When book distributors were not interested in handling the book, the Foxes sold it from home via mail order, and in toy shops.

The outcome

At one point, *The Beanie Baby Handbook* reached the number-two spot on the *New York Times* list of how-to paperback bestsellers, and Barnes and Noble reported that they were selling 20,000 copies a week. The total number sold is over 2 million. The cover price is $6.95, of which the Foxes net $1 per copy. They have also expanded into Beanie Baby cookbooks, CDs and trading cards.

The lessons

When a major phenomenon like the Beanie Babies occurs, it's possible to piggyback on to it profitably. Traditional producers and distributors may not see the opportunities, or may not be able to move quickly enough, which leaves the game open to small, independent businesses.

Of course there is the risk that the phenomenon will merely be a quickly passing fad, or will not attain the heights of success predicted for it. The latter happened with *Star Wars: Episode 1 – The Phantom Menace*. The publishers Dorling Kindersley vastly overestimated the number of spin-off books it could sell, and was left holding millions of unsold volumes. The financial impact resulted in the sale of the company.

Questions to ask yourself

1   Is there a phenomenon with which your business could have a natural synergy? This may be a product based on the phenomenon or one that is complementary in some way.

2   Can you piggyback without the permission of the producers of the original product? For example, if you had guessed that the film *Gladiator* was going to be a smash hit, you could have produced a book about the real history of gladiators, or produced gladiator action figures, but you could not have implied that these were directly related to the

film. If your idea does require permission, approach the producer about getting a licence to produce your spin-off or related product.

3 How long is the phenomenon likely to last? Even a hit film generally doesn't stay in the cinemas for more than a few months, so there would be a limited window of opportunity to piggyback on to it.

Tips: The art of piggybacking

1 Be sure you understand the phenomenon well. In the case of Les and Sue Fox, they invested in a complete set of Beanie Babies and followed all the related websites and toy magazines.

2 Brainstorm an aspect of the phenomenon that is not covered or is underdeveloped, and that could be taken advantage of quickly.

3 Try to control inventory so you don't end up with a warehouse full of items that are yesterday's news. As much as possible, stay only a little ahead of demand. This may mean sacrificing some economies of scale, but reduces risk.

Profit by association

The problem

To capitalise on the popularity of the name of Laura Ingalls Wilder. Wilder wrote the beloved *Little House on the Prairie* books which were the source of the Michael Landon TV series that ran in the United States and around the world.

The strategy

The writer TL Tedrow approached the publisher Thomas Nelson with the idea of writing a series of books with the general title *The Days of Laura Ingalls Wilder*. They would be fictional books with Wilder as the protagonist, and because she is a dead historical figure the Wilder estate does not have to give permission, nor does it get royalties (he could just as easily have written a series of fictional books entitled *The Days of Charles Dickens*, for example). The one legal limitation is that the dead person's name can't be used for promotional purposes (which means, for example, one couldn't market *Charles Dickens Cough Drops* without the permission of the Charles Dickens Estate). The publisher gave the idea the green light, and Tedrow wrote eight of the books.

The outcome

The publisher put a $500,000 promotion and advertising budget behind the series, and half a million copies of each book in the series were printed. However, Wilder's only heir protested, and called the books 'utter rip-off trash'. Tedrow admitted, 'I made up all the stories about her.'

The lessons

Piggybacking on a name and concept that are familiar to millions can be profitable (even though in this case the ethics may be questionable).

Questions to ask yourself

1   Are there well-known historical figures that might be used (ethically) to increase the familiarity of your product or business?
2   What other well-known elements might you be able to link with your product (for instance, a setting everyone is interested in, a historical incident, an out-of-copyright famous character from fiction)?

Tips: Piggybacking with the familiar

If you are considering a new name for your business, or a name for a new product, the following is a useful approach:

1   First list the qualities you would like people to associate with the business or product.
2   Next, generate a list of well-known historical people or places or things that are associated with the qualities you've listed.

3 Brainstorm how you could apply these terms to the product or business (and, if in doubt about the legality of using a name, check with a solicitor who specialises in copyright and trademark legislation).

Find partners

The problem

Two brothers, Dan and Tim Price, wanted to find ways to publicise and distribute their Send a Song service (the customer rings up and dictates a message to be sent to someone on their birthday, on St Valentine's Day or any other occasion, and a relevant song is played for them over the phone). But they wanted to do this in a way that didn't cost them money up front.

The strategy

The brothers came up with a three-pronged marketing plan.

1 The most important element is using radio. They license leading radio stations to attach their name to the Send a Song service locally. Listeners ring a toll-free number to take advantage of the 'KXYZ Send a Song Service'. The stations get a share of the revenue.

2 The brothers also worked out corporate tie-ins, in which people who buy a certain amount of product, for example, get a bonus of a free Send a Song coupon. The companies get a deep discount on the cost of the coupon, and the Send a Song company is introduced to a lot of new customers.

3 Finally, they also employ local distributors who work through gift and card shops and florists. Both the distributors and the stores get a percentage of the income from each coupon sold.

The outcome

The company sales figures doubled in one year and the service is set to expand.

The lessons

It can be very profitable to find partners who will do some of the work for you, in exchange for sharing in the profits. In this instance, the company could not afford to buy the radio advertising they're getting by making radio stations partners. In all three of the marketing and distribution channels they're using, they're sharing the work and the rewards, with minimal risk for all concerned.

Questions to ask yourself

1 Who are potential partners who could help you achieve your business goals?
2 How could you reward these partners with a share of profits, rather than having to pay up-front? (This also means, how can you get them to share in the risk?)

Tips: Finding partners

1 Begin by brainstorming all the types of businesses that deal with a similar customer base. If your products appeal primarily to young professionals, for example, what other businesses attract the attention of that group? Normally this would be non-competing businesses, but on occasion it may make sense for competitors to co-operate as well. One example is a group of restaurants all located in the same neighbourhood who could stage a joint publicity event to let people know the wealth of good dining available in that district.
2 Next, consider the ways potential partners could help you and, just as important, how you could benefit them. The case study gives several approaches. Others might include linking to each other's website, co-sponsoring an event that will attract the right demographic group, and sharing mailing lists.
3 Approach the most likely partners and suggest trying out the plan on a limited basis at first. This may overcome any initial suspicion or reservations they may have.

Find angels

The problem

When Michael Tod wrote his first novel, the publishers to whom he sent it liked it – but not enough to publish it. The book, *The Silver Tide*, is the story of how grey squirrels take over a community from red squirrels, and is set in Dorset, where the author grew up. Tod wanted to publish the book himself, but lacked money.

The strategy

Tod borrowed £4,000 from a relative to print 3,000 copies, and he persuaded twenty other people to invest in him and the book. He had them read the manuscript, and, in exchange for investing £245, each of them was promised 1 per cent of the profits from the book. Tod took copies of the book to bookshops in his area himself.

The outcome

Distributing the books himself, Tod managed to sell 1,100 of them in three weeks (cover price: £5). As a result, he was invited to be a guest on a BBC Radio Wales programme about publishing. There he met the chairman of a publishing firm, who paid him an advance of £10,000 for the trilogy of books of which *The Silver Tide* is the first. The deal includes another £10,000 if rights are sold in the United States. The initial print run is 6,000 in hardback, more than usual for a first novel. He has finished the rest of the trilogy and is working on another book.

The lessons

Tod was willing to take the risk of publishing the book himself, but he was also smart enough to spread the risk around by asking others to invest in him. Only the first investment was a fairly large one for an individual; the others were modest. Tod was businesslike about asking – he made the people shareholders in the book. Even if they didn't make any money this gave them a good dining-out story. He was also willing to do a lot of legwork: calling on local bookshops one by one is hard work. Certainly the meeting with the publisher on the radio show is something he couldn't have planned, but it's the sort of opportunity that often comes up when people are doing something different.

Questions to ask yourself

1 Have you considered how others might help you spread the risk of the cost of a project?
2 Have you considered ways in which to make other people's risk modest (no more than most people could afford to lose) and to make it businesslike?
3 Can you add an element of fun to other people's investment – a way, for example, to make them feel like backers or angels? Could you send them fancy-looking certificates or a fun annual report? Could you have a party that doubles as a shareholders' meeting?
4 What type of legwork could you do in order to get your project off the ground?
5 What types of publicity might you get to help your project? In the case of Michael Tod, the radio station initiated the contact with him, but often it's easy for the person with the project to contact the media.

Tips: Spreading the risk

1 Start with the people who know you best and are most likely to believe in you. Generally these will be family members, friends and colleagues. Do, however, give them an easy way to say no without causing bad feelings on either side.
2 Be honest with potential backers about the risks as well as the potential rewards.
3 Consult an accountant and a solicitor to make sure that any agreements you enter into are properly documented and are in accordance with tax regulations and other laws.
4 Keep backers informed of your progress and pay them back as soon as is practical. Send them copies of any newspaper or

magazine articles written about the venture – the more they feel involved, the more they will enjoy the process whether or not they ultimately make a profit.

Bring them together

The problem

The American ad agency GSD&M wanted to find ways to get greater publicity for their clients.

The strategy

They decided to find ways in which unlikely partners could benefit from being paired. For example, they painted a giant picture of Shamu, the killer whale at Anheuser-Busch's Sea World, on the side of a Southwest Airlines Boeing 737. Another example: they paired a US federal programme for rebuilding poor neighbourhoods with the National Basketball Association.

The outcome

GSD&M estimate that the Shamu-Southwest Airlines combination generated $12 million in free publicity. The NBA programme helped make inner-city residents aware of the federal funding available to them, and gave the NBA a positive image.

The lessons

Sometimes unlikely bedfellows turn out to be just the right partners. Bringing together non-competing businesses or a business with a charity or a government programme can generate a higher profile for both entities.

Questions to ask yourself

1 Could you partner your business with another one, or with a charity or a government agency, in a way that would create a win-win outcome?
2 Where can you network to meet the kind of people who might be open to this kind of suggestion?

3   Are you thinking laterally enough to come up with interesting and unexpected combinations?

Tips: Bringing yourself and them together

1   Begin by making a list of as many other types of businesses,
government agencies and charities as you can. Do not limit
yourself to those related to your field. In fact, eliminate any
that are in a similar field. A good way to generate this list is
just to flip through a volume of the Yellow Pages and note
the major categories.
2   Now brainstorm ways that your business and each of the
others might have something in common. Don't judge any
of these ideas: just jot them down – the more outrageous the
better. After all, who would have thought that an airline
would necessarily get excited about having a killer whale
portrayed on one of its planes?
3   When you've generated a lot of possibilities, go through
them to select the ones that would be a win-win proposition.
In other words, look for those that would benefit both participants.
4   Finally, of the remaining ideas, select the ones that you like
the most and that would generate the most publicity or give
the greatest benefit.

Power in numbers

The problem

A group of crime writers wanted to get more attention for their
work.

The strategy

Seven crime writers formed a group called Murder Squad. They
made their first public appearance at the opening of a Borders
bookstore. They also printed a full-colour brochure offering their
services for readings, workshops and talks at bookshops, libraries
and literature festivals.

The outcome

Although the group have not been together for long, they have garnered considerable publicity and have been invited to a variety of events at which they have promoted their books.

The lessons

Sometimes there is power in numbers where publicity is concerned. In this case, the group were smart enough to give newspaper and magazine editors a good visual: a group photo with the members dressed up in dark outfits and all wearing sunglasses, à la *Reservoir Dogs*. Even though each member cares most about promoting his or her books (the group consists of four men and three women), they recognised that a joint effort would pay off for them all.

Questions to ask yourself

1 What kind of publicity payoff might come from banding together with a group of similar businesses?
2 How could the group have visual appeal? Possibilities include a mascot, a common logo and a colourful outfit to be worn by employees.
3 Are there other benefits that could come from joining together – for example, discounts on bulk purchases made by the group?

Tips: Getting together

1 Consider all the factors that a group of businesses could have in common. These include geographical proximity, similarity of types of customers, similarity of products or services, and a charity or cause or sports team supported by all the businesses.
2 Be specific about the kind of publicity you want to get, and why. In the case of the writers, one was told by her publisher that, although she was getting good reviews, this wasn't translating into sales and she needed a higher public profile. In your case, you may want to get attention for a new

product or service, or to increase public awareness of one aspect of your business. Be clear about your goal.

3 Now see which of the factors of commonality would work best for the kind of publicity you want, and approach the appropriate other businesses whose needs may be in synch with yours.

4 When you have a group together, brainstorm what identity it can take, and how it can be given a visual value to appeal to the media.

One plus one make three

The problem

Coca-Cola wanted to find a new way to make their Diet Coke brand catch people's attention.

The strategy

They teamed up with several publishers and arranged to attach booklets to twelve- and twenty-four-packs of Diet Coke and caffeine-free Diet Coke. The booklets featured samples of the writing of popular authors, including Elmore Leonard and Barbara Taylor Bradford.

The outcome

A total of over 40 million such packages were distributed. Furthermore, Coke drinkers were asked to submit an essay on the topic of 'Living Life to the Fullest', and the winner was awarded an all-expenses-paid trip to New York for a meeting with an editor at a major publishing house. Also, the winner and 24 finalists had their essays put on the Diet Coke website.

The booklets appealed to the Diet Coke drinkers (a survey had shown that they tend to be better educated and more interested in reading than those who drink other soft drinks), and the company reported a positive response from their customers.

The authors donated their work in exchange for the publicity, and they and the publishers were delighted to reach such a wide audience – one that might then buy books by the writers in question.

Also, the unusual nature of the promotion meant it got a lot of press coverage for all the partners.

The lessons

This case study is a good example of a combination that is not necessarily the most logical, but worked very well. In fact, sometimes the very fact that a pairing is unusual makes it newsworthy and increases its chances of success.

Questions to ask yourself

1 Who might you partner with in order to spread the word of your product or service?
2 What unusual combinations can you think of that perhaps have never been used before in your type of business?

Tips: Successful odd-couple partnerships

1 If you haven't already done so in the previous exercise, jot down a list of all the types of businesses and products that come to mind.
2 For each one, consider whether and how it might combine with your business or product. Could either of you attach or include or give away a sample of the other's product? Could you give their customers discounts and have them give your customers a discount?
3 For each combination that seems promising, consider the payoff for each partner. There must be a payoff for both sides, whether that is finding new customers, winning valuable publicity, or something else.

Use the power of multiple strategies

All of the strategies you have read about so far are fantastic ways to turbocharge your marketing effort. Now imagine the power of combining several of them at one time!

When you have selected which of these principles you are going to apply, check whether you can combine them in new ways. The effect may well be not to double or triple the effectiveness of your marketing efforts, but to make them ten times as powerful. The following case studies illustrate how this works.

Solve problems

The problem

American parents and educators were finding it difficult to find biographies of black men and women.

The strategy

Three black women established a company, Black Books Galore, to hold book fairs and festivals offering children's books about black people, Native Americans and other cultures. They did mailings to schools, and they arranged to be interviewed in the press.

The outcome

In the first year of operation, the company held book fairs and festivals in over a dozen cities and received requests from all over the United States to do the same. Their line of books received local, national and international coverage, and has sold well.

The lessons

The founders of the company started with a need they had themselves: to find good books about different ethnic groups. They felt that, if *they* had this need, so must many others. This is often an effective starting point for establishing a new business.

Rather than expecting the potential customers to find them, the company founders went out to find the customers by travelling to black and multiethnic communities. Going where the customers are – finding them instead of hoping they will find you – is always a good strategy as well. They then went to another logical point of interest for such books, schools and libraries. They also used the power of publicity.

Questions to ask yourself

1. Are there consumer needs you have that are not being fulfilled, and that you think others must have as well? Have you come up with a product or service that can fulfil these needs?
2. If you have an elusive target population, is there a way you can take your product or service to them rather than wait for them to come to you?
3. Can you combine these strategies into a newsworthy marketing campaign?

Tips: Giving people what they need

1. Start with your own needs. Forget for a moment about what things are like currently or what seems possible and daydream about what you, as a customer, would want ideally from the kind of business or service you provide.
2. Extend this questioning to your friends and colleagues.

Encourage them to think in terms of the ideal, and not be limited by the current.

3 With a list of these wishes, brainstorm how you could meet some of them. What changes would you have to make? What resources would you require? What new ways of thinking would help?

A little sugar . . .

The problem

Kenneth Kramm, a marketing man, wanted to come up with a way to help his father, the owner of a local pharmacy, be competitive with the big chains of chemists.

The strategy

Noticing that his own young daughter hated taking strong-tasting medicine, Kramm asked his father for help. They added flavouring to the medicine and the little girl found it much more palatable. Eventually they offered a variety of flavours to customers who had prescriptions for medication for their children, and charged an extra fee per prescription to add a shot of the flavouring.

The outcome

The flavourings were so popular that customers came from far and wide, and the Kramms decided to license the flavourings to other chemists (but not to the big chains). For an initial fee, each chemist receives recipes, a flavouring kit and advertising and marketing schemes. Thereafter, there is an annual fee. In the first two years, 350 chemists signed up. The Kramms then began work on a flavouring system for over-the-counter medicines and one geared to geriatric patients.

The lessons

As in the previous case study, a breakthrough idea began with a problem faced by the inventor. When the Kramms came up with a solution to their own problem, they realised it would probably also appeal to others. By deciding to limit the sales of their mixtures to independent drugstores, they gave those stores a unique product – one that the major chains could not offer. This made their product more valuable to these customers. They then realised that they could multiply their success by extending the product to other groups of customers, such as elderly people.

Questions to ask yourself

1   Is there a problem you have solved for yourself that might also give you the idea for a product or service that would appeal to others?
2   Is there a way you could restrict your product or service to one niche in a way that would make it extra appealing to those customers?
3   Is there a way your product or service could be extended to serve other niche target groups?

Tips: Adding a spoonful of sugar

1   Ask your customers, informally or formally, what are the worst problems they face. You may think you know this already, but you may be surprised. If the buyers of your product are not the end users, try to get input from the people who are. For example, someone supplying bags to a chain of supermarkets might ask the checkout operators as well as the purchasing agents.
2   Brainstorm ways that you might solve some of the problems you hear about.
3   If you cannot solve the problem, brainstorm ways to lessen its impact. In our example, the children still had to take the medicine, but the Kramms made it a less unpleasant experience. Perhaps there is a negative experience faced by your customers that you can make less unpleasant. (For example, someone who has a dental practice could make the experience of waiting more pleasant by playing comedy videotapes on a monitor, or having headphones for each chair so people could listen to their choice of music, or providing Nintendo-style games.)

Make it memorable

The problem

When starting a computer resale company, Don Mayer wanted to come up with a way to make his company stand out.

The strategy

Mayer decided to give his company a unique name: Small Dog Electronics. He based this not only on the novelty value of the name, but also on the fact that, in this large field, he is a 'small dog', and he's also a dog lover.

He didn't stop at the name. He also created a Top Dog Club for customers, and a newsletter he called *Kibbles and Bytes*, which goes to the 40,000 members of the clubs.

He also installed three 'DogCams', which visitors to his website (SmallDog.com) can use to see his business premises (and maybe catch a glimpse of his dogs).

The outcome

Mayer reports that the strategy has been hugely successful in attracting customers and getting them to come back. The dog-lover theme seems to be a potent one: hundreds of customers have even submitted photos of their pets to be posted on the SmallDog.com site.

The lessons

Mayer has used the multiple-strategy approach. By giving his company an unusual name he attracts potential customers by arousing their curiosity. By carrying the theme through, he entertains the customers. By offering them membership in his club and sending them a diverting newsletter, he gives them something for nothing and in effect makes them partners as well as customers.

Questions to ask yourself

1 Have you established an identity that stands out from those of your competitors in the marketplace?

2 Do you carry through your identity in a variety of ways?

3 Do you use a mix of strategies to attract and keep customers?

Tips: Bringing in and keeping customers

1 If you feel that your company is getting lost in the shuffle of competitors, consider rebranding it. Naturally this is not a decision to be taken lightly, as it will require a variety of tasks and expenses (accounting and legal expenses, new letterhead and business cards and so forth) and could be confusing for your current customers. However, it can also mean a burst of new energy as well as a lasting higher profile.

2 Don't limit yourself to pursuing only one of the strategies in this book. Make one of them the centrepiece, then consider how others could be added or combined. For example, if you decide to give something away to attract customers (Principle 6), also consider how the giveaway could be made newsworthy (Principle 9), whether the distribution of the free item might be more effective if you team up with a partner company (Principle 13), and how you can use the process to enhance the customer's perception of your company (Principle 7).

Use every means

The problem

American Lorie Line had a job as a director of marketing for a large company but hated it. She wanted to find a way to make a living with music.

The strategy

Line successfully applied to play piano during evenings and weekends in a department store. She collected the names and addresses of customers who came up to her and asked if she had an album. She then recorded an album and persuaded the department store manager to allow her to sell her tapes and CDs while she played. She quit her job and also started playing at parties. She approached record companies, but they were not interested, so instead she approached small gift shops. She then persuaded ten small distribution companies to carry her records, and she scheduled concerts in towns where her CDs and tapes were selling well.

The outcome

Eventually, the Musicland chain (800 stores) and several other major store chains agreed to carry her product. She now has fourteen albums, a 'recorded-live' CD and a public television special that has been seen by 30 million people. Her sales total $4.5 million, and her husband has quit his job to be her tour manager.

The lessons

Lorie Line sums up the lessons this way: 'Decide what you want to do, calculate the risks, figure out what you could lose, then take a chance! … If somebody tells you no, you're talking to the wrong person.'

Questions to ask yourself

1   If you have a new business, product or service, what are the small beginnings that might lead to greater things? Where can you get initial attention?
2   Do you have a diversity of marketing strategies in mind?

Tips: Using every means

1   Lorie Line started small and allowed her enterprise to grow, using a variety of marketing approaches. Certainly playing the piano in a department store is not the usual path to a successful recording career. Are there small beginnings you have considered but rejected because they were unusual? If so, revisit them now and decide whether some of them may be worth exploring after all.
2   Line also followed a very logical path in the expansion of the business she loved. Draw a chart of how you'd like your business to grow, following a similar line of logic. Then translate each step into a series of tasks and schedule them one by one.

Find them everywhere

The problem

Michael Dweck, an advertising man, wanted to find new ways of connecting his investment-seeking clients with venture capitalists.

The strategy

Dweck learned about the day of an average venture capitalist in order to map out a variety of low-cost ways his clients could get to them. For example, he found out which delicatessens on California Street in San Francisco are the favoured lunchtime hangouts of venture capitalists, and arranged for his clients' ads to be pasted on to the lunch delivery bags.

Another example: he hired actors to go to favourite VC bars and pretend to talk on mobile phones, saying interesting things about his clients, so the VCs could overhear the conversations.

The outcome

According to Dweck, his stunts have led to one of his clients getting a $35 million investment.

The lessons

It's always good to have alternative strategies for getting to the people you want to reach. If they won't see you in their offices, perhaps you can figure out other places to reach them. The same could apply to potential customers, of course. It may be that no one strategy has the desired effect by itself, but in combination they reach a critical mass.

Questions to ask yourself

1. If you are not reaching potential clients or customers using the traditional channels, have you thought of an array of alternatives?
2. How could you apply Dweck's kind of guerrilla marketing techniques to your business?

Tips: Many paths lead to the same destination

1 Identify any customer groups that you are not reaching effectively enough using traditional methods.

2 Brainstorm how many other ways you could reach them, using their daily schedule as a guide. For example, where do they eat breakfast, lunch and dinner? How do they get to work? Are there after-work pubs or restaurants or coffee shops where they tend to stop off before going home? How do they spend their evenings? Your goal is to generate a large number of possibilities.

3 For each guerrilla approach you come up with, make sure that it is legal and not more likely to annoy the potential clients than to win them over.

It all adds up

The problem

When the theatre producer Cameron Mackintosh decided to move the musical *Five Guys Named Moe* from the fringe theatre Stratford East, to the more formal West End, he wanted to be sure the production kept its free-and-easy atmosphere.

The strategy

Mackintosh sat down with the director at Stratford East, Philip Hedley, and asked what made the atmosphere there so lively, compared with the sober atmosphere of West End theatres. One factor was that the Stratford East ushers were younger and jollier, so Mackintosh moved the usual West End ushers to another theatre and brought in younger ushers. Another element was that typical West End prices tend to deter younger audiences, so Mackintosh charged only £3 for tickets in the gallery. Typically, West End audiences are more polite and reserved, so he hired a meeter and greeter to joke with the audience as they came into the foyer. Also he had the cast members lead the audience in a conga to the bar at the interval.

The outcome

The musical had excellent word-of-mouth and ran for four years in the West End.

The lessons

Mackintosh began by considering all of the factors that would help create the result he wanted, and then implemented them one by one. The key was looking at a variety of factors that would add up to the desired result. This can be done with any product or service.

Questions to ask yourself

1 What are the individual elements of your product or service that will add up to making the impression you want?
2 Are there other elements you could add in order to create an overall effect?

Tips: Making it all add up

1 Begin by considering how you want the customer or client to feel about your product or service. In our example, Mackintosh wanted the audience to feel in a good mood, playful and ready to participate as well as to watch.
2 Brainstorm all the factors that might contribute to the customers perceiving your product or service in the way you would like them to. This might include the packaging, the advertising, the nature of their interaction with your receptionist and so on.
3 Brainstorm how you could modify each of these factors in order to increase the likelihood that your customer will have the ideal experience.

The path to a bestseller

The problem

George Gibson, publisher at Walker and Company in the United States, wanted to make a bestseller out of a nonfiction science history book – until then not normally the kind of book found on the bestseller lists.

The strategy

Gibson followed a multipronged strategy. He decided to target independent bookstores, reasoning that the big chains would come on board if they could see that the book was selling well elsewhere. First he made thousands of proof copies that were designed to look like the finished product, and he gave away 1,300 of them at the American Booksellers' Association convention. Next, he approached Patrick O'Brian, a very successful historical novelist, for a quote about the book. He had the book's author, Dava Sobel, inscribe messages on four hundred copies, which he posted to influential retailers. He spent about $50,000 on these and related activities (the author's advance had been less than $25,000).

The outcome

The book, *Longitude*, became a Book of the Month Club selection and was picked up by all the major book chains. It received a favourable review in the *New York Times*, and National Public Radio interviewed the author. The book did get on to the *New York Times* bestseller list, and stayed there for months. It also became a hot seller in gift and speciality shops as well as bookstores in America and the United Kingdom, and has been translated into several languages.

The lessons

Gibson designed a multipronged strategy, so that if any of the elements didn't happen as he wished (for example, if Patrick O'Brian had not come up with a laudatory quote, although he did), the other parts of the marketing plan would still be in place. He also took a major risk financially because he was convinced that the book had huge potential and its success would help the visibility not only of the author but also of the publishing house. No risk – no reward.

Questions to ask yourself

1 Have you considered using the power of endorsements as part of your marketing plan?

2 Have you used the personal touch (in our case study, the inscribed books) in connecting more closely with potential clients or customers?

3 Have you taken full advantage of trade fairs and conventions in order to reach your customers?

Tips: Making a bestseller (not only books)

1 Brainstorm whose endorsement might help you win over new customers. Specify well-known individuals in your field, and also *types* of individuals (for example, for a cookery book, endorsements from several chefs could be valuable, even if the chefs are not famous).

2 Brainstorm how you might get these people to endorse your product or service. Often the publicity they get in the form of a quote and perhaps their photo in an ad or in your promotional material is enough of a reward.

3 Brainstorm how you could add the personal touch to making contact with key potential customers. This might include writing a personal note from you or from one of the workers who make the product, for example, or simply including a photo of the staff behind the product or service.

How to Brainstorm

A lot of the tips following the case studies in this book suggest that you do some brainstorming in order to come up with ways to adapt different marketing strategies to your business. Brainstorming doesn't mean just sitting around trying to think of ideas: it's a specific process with its own guidelines and procedures, which are easy to learn. In this chapter, we'll show you exactly how to do it.

First, though, let's get rid of one misconception: that only artists and select others are creative. The fact is, we all start out creative – can you think of a five-year-old who is not creative? We lose it along the way, deadened by rote learning, by well-intentioned parents who fear that we'll get into trouble and by a society that discourages people from asking too many inconvenient questions.

For a long time, adult creativity was thought to be the exclusive province of writers and artists – certainly it was seldom spoken of in the context of business. Now that it is increasingly recognised that ideas are the new currency of business, surely this has changed. Or has it? In his book *The Tom Peters Seminar* the eponymous management guru writes, 'Even our new theories of management steadfastly ignore the issues of creativity and zest.'

For most people (and companies), creativity remains an abstract notion: they'd like to have more of it, but they're not sure how to get it, or what to do with it once they have it. First, let's consider the goal of applied creativity: what will it help you to do?

The goal: do something different

Who are the people in your field that you admire? Most likely, they are in some way pioneers, people who came up with something new, or a new way to present something old. We study what such people do, but generally what we are taught to copy is their outcome, not the process they used to reach their outcome. The result is that we become good imitators, but don't ourselves come up with breakthrough ideas.

Furthermore, it's not enough to do something different just once. It used to be enough to present something new and then exploit it for one's lifetime; nowadays, a successful career requires several changes of direction. In show business, David Bowie and Madonna are two experts at keeping up public interest by periodically changing their images and how they do what they do.

This principle applies not only to show business, but to all other fields, including computers and new media, fashion, even manufacturing (for example, the changes that will be demanded in car design and production over the next twenty years will dwarf the changes that have taken place in the last seventy).

Management gurus such as Tom Peters stress that the saying 'If it ain't broke, don't fix it' no longer applies. By the time you notice that it's broken (or no longer of interest to the customers) it's too late. You have to anticipate the end of the life term of what you are offering if you want to be part of the next wave.

In a moment we'll explore some specific creativity techniques you can use to discover how to be different in a way that makes a difference. If it's been a while since you've used your creative mind, you may experience some blocks, so first let's look at what these are – and how to remove them.

What stops you from being more creative?

The block

Going too fast to have new ideas. The pressure to get results fast means that people no longer take the time to stop and reflect. After all, someone who's just sitting around, staring into space, isn't working, right?

The solution

Take time to think. The momentum of old ideas and familiar techniques must be interrupted. If you can't do this at your desk, take a walk or hide in an empty conference room (take along a notepad or small tape recorder to capture your ideas). Leave behind all the usual approaches and solutions.

Play for a while to free your mind. This can be purely mental (how long has it been since you've looked up at the clouds to see which animals they resemble?) or you can use a yo-yo, or a pen and pad to doodle. Then, still in that relaxed frame of mind and with no urgency, consider the problem at hand to see what new ideas emerge.

The block

Fear of failure. Any time we follow a new direction, we risk. In the business world, risk is rewarded – if the result is positive. If not, it can mean losing your job. So how can you risk and yet be sure of winning? You can't. (Sorry.)

The solution

Get inspired. As Suzanne Merritt, senior creatologist for Polaroid, said in an interview, 'Stifled creativity is particularly evident in the corporate world where executives are terrified of getting off the track to success. They've been trained to follow the rules rather than making them up.'

At the same time, it's clear that the true breakthroughs come from the rule breakers. Read the biographies of people you admire in your field, whether it's Picasso, Richard Branson,

Marie Curie or Winston Churchill. Notice how these people embraced risk, and then apply their way of thinking to your situation. Also, be aware of how many of the true pioneers experienced several failures before they made their stunning breakthroughs.

The block

Fear of confusion. Making changes a little at a time is comfortable – but not the stuff of breakthroughs. The big changes that come with revolutionary ideas require walking on the edge, not knowing from moment to moment how things are going.

The solution

Faith. A few decades ago, a troubled woman went to a famous healer, and she said, 'I am so in the dark. How long must I be in the dark?' The healer thought about it for a moment, then replied, 'Until you can see in the dark.' The faith we're talking about is not faith that you're doing the right thing every moment, but faith that every experience is a learning experience, and that your mistakes can be used to correct your course so that eventually you end up in the right place. It's faith in yourself, in your flexibility.

The block

Resistance from other people. When we first suggest something new, the most likely response is resistance. Even when the old ways aren't working so well, they're 'the devil you know', and that makes them comfortable. You may find others trying to block your new path at first.

The solution

Communication. If you have heroes or heroines in your field, the odds are that, as well as being brilliant at what they did, they were excellent communicators. As Don Tornberg, vice-president of Progress for Amoco, said in *Fast Company* magazine, 'You need to change people's mind-sets and behaviour. It's psychological as well as methodological.' In other words, mere facts aren't enough. You need to make it easy for people to buy into your ideas with minimum risk for them. For a wealth of ideas on how to do this, see the book *Influence*, by Robert Cialdini.

Get out of the box!

Now that you have seen some ways of opening up to your own creativity, let's look at specific techniques you can use to generate new ideas.

In my workshops, we do a lot of small-group exercises, but you can also brainstorm by yourself. In both situations, the same simple guidelines apply:

1 The more ideas the better.
2 No judging! This is not the time to evaluate ideas, and, if you start criticising yourself or others, it will stop the free flow of ideas.
3 Write everything down.
4 Don't be afraid to build on or suggest a twist to a previous idea. Sometimes a small change is all it takes to turn an ordinary idea (or product) into an outstanding one.

I suggest that you have a challenge in mind as you try out each of the following creativity exercises.

One plus one makes three

Generate a list of fifteen random words (or use fifteen images from magazines). Relate each to the problem – what ideas does each one prompt?

For example, let's say the challenge is getting journalists to read your press releases, and the word you use is 'oxygen'. Free-associate how these two might connect: 'Oxygen is about breathing, it also reminds me of those masks that come down in aeroplanes in an emergency – maybe we could do the press release in the form of one of those laminated emergency cards you find in the seat pocket of an aeroplane.'

Notice that the first word is just a starting point. Your free association may take you far away from the original word, and that's fine. Generate and write down at least twenty or thirty ideas before you start judging them.

 ## Meet the Martian

Pretend you have to explain the situation to a Martian. How does reducing it to its simplest elements help suggest a solution? This is related to the Zen notion of 'beginner's mind', the fact that often we know so much about a situation that we cannot see it as clearly as a beginner who is free of preconceptions.

Solving the puzzle

Make a list of everything that will be different when the problem is solved. Now consider each item separately and tackle them one by one.

Let's take an example from personal life. If the problem is that the relationship with a spouse or partner is feeling stale, what would the solution look like? When the problem is solved, the two people might communicate more at breakfast, they might take more trips together, they might share more personal issues, they might give each other small but meaningful presents the way they used to.

What if one partner took the initiative and started addressing one of these aspects – for example, making a point of not rushing off in the mornings, but taking time to have breakfast and maybe even serving the partner breakfast in bed sometimes?

Small changes in one aspect of a situation often start a shift in the larger problem. If you work towards a change in each of the components, you will reach a point of critical mass, and the entire problem will disappear.

 ## Fantasy island

Take five minutes to daydream that you journey to an island or a mountaintop and ask the advice of the world's wisest woman or man. What does she or he say? To make this work, take your time and in your imagination really see, hear and feel the fantasy world you enter. Don't force answers, just allow them to happen. If none come the first time, maybe the wisest person in the world is out to lunch. Try again later.

The history lesson

Think of a time when you handled a major challenge well. List the attributes that made you effective that time. Consider how each of these could be applied to your current challenge.

One thing these techniques have in common is that they are playful. Indeed, our creativity workshops are always full of laughter and fun, even when the problems being dealt with are serious. When participants come up with exciting solutions, they have not only solved a problem, but have begun to see themselves in a different way. After your first few successes at rediscovering your creativity, you may find you've also gained additional confidence in general.

William James, the father of modern psychology, wrote: 'I have no doubt that most people live, whether physically, intellectually, or morally, in a very restricted circle of their potential being ... We all have reservoirs of life to draw upon, of which we do not dream.'

Your creativity is one such reservoir. If you would like more practical guidelines to being more creative, I'd be happy to send you our free monthly creativity e-bulletin (we never sell or share our subscribers' names). Just email your name and email address to us at BstormUK@aol.com. You can also see our website, www.BrainstormNet.com, for more creativity techniques and suggested resources.

Once you make a habit of using your creativity, you will find that it will give you an endless flow of ideas for your business life and your personal life, and that it will enrich both beyond measure. One excellent way to apply your creativity, of course, is to come up with your own marketing plan. First, in the next chapter, you'll hear how the professionals do it. Then, in the following chapter, you'll find guidelines for doing it yourself.

The Pros' View of Marketing

To give you an idea of how professional marketing companies approach their task, I interviewed two outstanding representatives of the world of marketing. The first interview is with Lizz Clarke, the head of LCM, which was established in 1988, initially as the outsource of a US-based company. Having put them firmly on the map, the company developed four core-skills areas which they now offer to an increasing number of national and international organisations. The four core areas are marketing consultancy and public relations; professional writing; graphic design; and marketing-related training. LCM is a good example of a smaller marketing company, in that it has a core staff of about half a dozen but uses a large number of specialist freelancers to provide whatever a client might need. LCM's clients include Business Telecom Systems Ltd., Trethowans Solicitors, the National Sales Awards, and the charity Wateraid.

Lizz, let's start with something very basic. How do you define marketing?

I define it as the whole process of creating something that is then going to be bought by an individual, or a group of people, or another company. You're then creating an image and an awareness of it in the minds of the target group.

Let's say someone comes to you and says they have a product or service they would like to market. How do you proceed?

The first thing we would do is ask people lots of questions and really find out in detail not just what the product is and what it can do, but also where are they now, and what's their dream of where they want to be. It's terribly important that we use that energy and their excitement about it in order to make it work. If they don't have that excitement about their product, frankly, we will not work with them.

Probably the hardest question we ask them is, 'Who will buy this product or service? Who is it meant for? Who is the target audience?' Often they want to say 'everybody' but, if it's for everybody, then it's not for anybody in particular and it's impossible to reach everybody. Therefore we would work with them to identify a segment of the population that would most need or appreciate this product. For example, one client recently came to us with a very low budget and we suggested they think only of graduates coming out of university as their target market, and that is working very well.

Once we've found out the clients' goals, we ask what kind of ideas they already have. Very often the clients' ideas are very good and they are using us because they think we'll have a magic answer nobody else could possibly think of. Of course sometimes we've come up with unique solutions, but normally it's just a discipline that we're following and getting the client to follow. We're making them spend the time, we're making them spend the money, we're making them spend the effort and energy that they wouldn't have spent if we hadn't been there.

One of the crucial elements is the image of the product, how it should be represented to the target audience. We give the product a look and put some words to it that say very clearly what it is they're trying to say.

I like to look at the things we create as marketing assets. For example, if I have taken some photographs of the directors or some of the team working together, I can use that in a newspaper for public relations, I can use it on a website as a picture of a team, I can use it on a CD-ROM, or put it on a poster. Our clients have smaller budgets, so I like to make their money go a long way.

How else might you use these assets?

These days you can tell a whole sales story on a website; there might be a telesales campaign, a mailshot, advertising, and a variety of public relations efforts. We want the look and feel of the product to be consistent all the way across these efforts.

Since we are talking about doing something different, what are some of the more unusual approaches you use?

We get their name and photograph into the local press so they get to be known to the local audience. We like them to give talks to local businesses and go to events where they can network.

One slightly unusual thing we do is to look for who will really be the best representative or spokesperson for them. It's not always the leaders of the company.

Who else might it be?

For example, on my rounds of one firm of solicitors, I found a fantastic receptionist who makes a wonderful spokesperson. At an international private college we work with, I found a top student, Alex, who is the best spokesperson you could imagine. Don't get me wrong: the headmistress is fantastic; so is the deputy head. But this boy loves the college and is totally enthusiastic. He has no vested interest in selling the place, so, when he talks about how great it is, people know that he's sincere and they get a sense of what it's really like to be there.

Sometimes I will coach clients who are not so comfortable speaking in a group, and I encourage them not to be afraid to do something unusual. For example, last week I attended a function of seventy people, and the chairman couldn't get them to sit down for the lunch, so I just shouted, 'Shut up!' Everybody turned around and thought, Who is this woman? And when they saw the smile on my face they knew it was good-natured and they chuckled and shut up and sat down. I tell clients not to be afraid to get noticed.

Of course not everybody would feel comfortable shouting 'Shut up!' at a group, even in a joking way.

No, and it's very important that people market themselves to be exactly who they are and to be honest about what their product can and can't do. If in doubt, undersell rather than overpromise. But, within that, we can have fun, too. Marketing has a serious purpose, but it works better when everybody enjoys themselves, so why not be a bit playful when that's appropriate?

Do you have any more examples of doing something different?

There's one we're doing right now that I can't talk about too much, but let's say that we're using one section of the newspaper, the classified ads, to get attention for a client. These ads are very inexpensive, but, if you can use them to create a buzz around a person or product, they can really pay off.

Sometimes we have clients take a fresh look at how they are using their current resources. For example, almost everybody prints brochures, but I get passionately cross when they don't use the brochures properly. I tell the client I'm going to need fifteen minutes of all the staff's time. We go and talk to a few people first so we know we're talking the right cultural language, and then we create a presentation on how to use the brochures. We ask them questions and make it quite interactive. I think that's a bit uncommon for smaller companies like ours.

You mentioned that you work primarily with small to medium-sized companies and maybe some individuals as well; is there a rough guideline regarding the size of the marketing and PR budgets you deal with?

We have dealt with a range, but these days it's unusual for us to take on somebody who has a budget of less than twenty thousand pounds a year.

Occasionally we will work with people on a different basis. For example, a group called the Business Network has asked us to prepare three press releases for them per year, in exchange for membership in their club. Frankly, we will lose a bit of money on it, but

I'm sending my staff along to their networking meetings and just last week one met a portrait photographer there, who we will use as a supplier. She also met someone looking for PR and marketing representation, who may become a new client.

Can you offer some advice for people who may not have enough money to hire a service such as yours and will be handling the marketing function themselves?

I would say the first thing to do is specify your goals. Be very, very clear on what you're trying to achieve. Start by going right back to the most basic question: are you in the right business? If you're not really happy in what you're doing and aren't clear on what you're trying to achieve, I think you may be in the wrong business and you won't have the energy to do what you will need to do in terms of marketing. You won't have the confidence and determination to go out there and sell yourself.

But assuming you're excited about what you're doing, once you have your goals clear, decide on a strategy. You will know who you want to reach, and you should have many routes for reaching them.

One route might be a public relations push to get known in your trade media or local media. Others might be advertising, direct mail, phone calls and networking. I always encourage networking, as that is the least expensive and often the most effective.

Decide on your strategy and stick with it. Give it a good six months to a year to see if it's working. You can adjust the strategy, but don't get diverted. Often people are very impatient, they forget that it takes time to have an impact so they move to doing something else just before what they were doing was about to pay off.

You should test and measure the results of what you are doing. If you are doing a direct-mail campaign, send out two or three different letters. Send each one to a hundred people and see which one gives you the best results.

Dare to pick up the phone and talk to potential customers. My guideline for this is, if I can't think of any genuine way I'm going to help this businessperson's life, I shouldn't be making this phone call. You've got to sit there and focus on what you can do for them, and then your whole voice changes, your attitude changes, and they accept you.

Any advice for dealing with the press?

What I've just said, about win-win situations, even works with newspaper editors, who can be a bit severe on the phone sometimes. Yes, they get lots of people wanting their attention, but they are also trying to fill up column inches, so call them and concisely tell them what you have to offer. If you have something they want, both of you will benefit.

What editors want is new information that will interest readers. Write a headline that will catch the editor's attention, not the reader's. If you're writing for the Bolton *Evening News*, if it has a Bolton businessperson in the headline, that will grab an editor's attention, whereas, if the headline is SOUTHAMPTON COMPANY DOES SUCH AND SUCH, that will not be interesting.

Put the most important information at the start of the story, not the end. Most clients fail to do this when they write their own press releases.

If you can possibly afford to do so, do pay someone to write good copy for you and do good graphics for you – those are good investments. That applies to sales letters as well.

Finally, one general piece of advice: be as open as you possibly can be as a person to opportunity; don't put barriers up. Be positive towards other people and welcoming towards other people. If you are excited about what you are offering, if you are convinced that your product or service will help people or delight them, that will come across, and that is the most important bit of marketing you could possibly do.

Thank you. If people want to contact you, how should they do it?

At lizz@lcm.co.uk or via our website, www.lcm.co.uk

*   *   *

The next interview is with Craig Newman, CEO of Mediator Marketing, a much larger London-based company (between forty and fifty staff) with an impressive client list. Mediator has worked with Carphone Warehouse, Virgin Cola and the Mirror Group, among many others. Although they are a larger agency, they pride themselves on personal service, as Craig Newman explains.

At Mediator, how do you define marketing?

At Mediator we look at the communication of brand to the consumer. We, as an agency, are media-neutral. We won't say automatically we'll do sales promotion; we won't say we will do advertising; we won't say we will run a direct marketing campaign. We'll take the perspective of, 'This is the brand and that's the consumer. How do we best communicate that brand to that consumer?'

In the last few years, business books and articles in the business press have been saying that branding is more important than ever before. Do you agree with that?

I do think that branding is becoming increasingly important. People are being bombarded with more and more messages as technology improves and increases. The source of information on products or services is vast: newspapers, TV, the Internet, magazines, mobile phones, PDAs [personal digital assistants], email and more besides.

If you are a company and you are trying to market your product, there are many different ways to target the consumer. But the only way of actually making sure that you get your message across is to build a very strong brand.

I think, in terms of how the City views companies, there is a global value for brands. Across the world people see a brand and feel comforted by it.

Does that make life difficult for the smaller and medium-size companies, to have to compete in that way, without the resources of a Coca-Cola or a McDonald's?

I think there is always a way if you are innovative. Even if you have huge amounts of money it doesn't necessarily mean you are going to be successful in terms of the work that you do behind that brand.

When we worked with Virgin Cola they always used to say Coca-Cola had ten times as much money to spend, therefore we need to be ten times as effective and therefore ten times as creative. And that's what we as an agency believe: if you are very creative and you do look at things cleverly, there are always ways of competing with the big boys.

I suppose, depending on what your market niche is, you don't need to get worldwide recognition or even total national recognition: you need to get the brand known within the group of people to whom you are appealing.

Absolutely, there is no reason you need to be talking to people who aren't relevant to your brand. Saga are a very successful company within the over-fifty-fives marketplace, they talk to that market, they are not talking to a twenty-five-year-old or thirty-year-old.

Given that we have had a shake-out in companies on the Internet, how much of an impact does the Internet have on marketing, and how do you see the future in that regard?

I think we are at just the beginning of the Internet. We as an agency always believed that the Internet is another channel, another way of communicating to the consumer.

What you see now is that the well-funded and well-run start-ups are ploughing on, they are strong enough to survive, and the ones that are second-tier or badly run are struggling.

The big companies that have financial muscle are coming in. Either they are buying a company that is about to go to the water, to give them access to the Internet and to that technology, or they are looking at relationships that might be mutually beneficial.

The clients we work with are the companies that we believe will be there in the long term.

Does the client come to you with an image already in mind they want to pursue, or is it part of your job to help them find that?

With most new clients, we will do what we call a 'Mediator 360', which is looking at the business, looking at the brand, looking at the consumer and looking at the challenges of communicating that brand to the consumer.

Some companies are much further advanced: they have very detailed knowledge of what they think their brand is. One of the biggest problems we have in the industry is that managers often perceive the brand as being very different to how the consumer actually perceives the brand. What we try to do as an agency is take one step back, to make sure the perceptions are accurate.

Our mission statement is very much about questioning everything, so that we can deliver outstanding communications solutions. As a business we question everything that our clients do as a company, so that we can create the most effective way to achieve their objectives.

Can you talk us through the whole process you would normally go through when a company comes to you?

Let me give you an example. Two industrialists who run engineering companies came to us with a product they were looking at launching and a concept that we as an agency believed in. If we didn't believe in it, we would say it wasn't for us and wouldn't take it forward.

We started with the 'Mediator 360', at the very beginning of the business cycle. We look at where their business sits and in what kind of context to the marketplace. We go through the process of looking at every element of the business. We look at the competition and the potential growth areas. We say where we think they should be taking the business. In short, we look at every aspect of their business.

Then it's the brand's turn. We look at what that brand consists of, the facets of that brand, its personality, its tone of voice. Then we look at the consumer groups and who would be relevant for that brand.

For the company I'm using as an example, there were two distinct groups: twenty-five-to-thirty-five-year-olds, who have large disposable incomes and are interested in something that is very exciting; the second audience was the corporate sales directors that would want to use this product as a reward for their sales teams.

Then we looked at ways of communicating the brand to those two groups of people.

After that we write a report indicating the way we believe the process should go forward, how we would propose to work with the company.

When a company comes to you, what sort of time commitment do you ask them for, in order to implement the plans that you both agree on?

For us to do a 360 will normally take us at least two days of preparation and a one-day workshop session between their management team and ours.

Then we will want a couple of days to write a report. It's about a week's worth of time, which usually takes place over a two-week period. That's stage one.

Stage two will normally be three months for either research, or research and communication-strategy development. At the end of that period we will be ready to implement a plan that covers the next six to nine months.

What are the channels you use for reaching different target groups of consumers?

We use every possible channel. We're an integrated agency. As I said earlier, we look at the brand first and the medium second. That way we don't force-feed our clients. We never create ads because we're an ad agency. Or direct marketing because that's what we do. No, we take a holistic approach, of which our 360 is just the first step. Ultimately, we create an integrated campaign based on a single, persuasive idea that should or could be applied everywhere: advertising, direct marketing, new media, sales promotion, in every channel. It's about creating a dialogue with the customer and continuously enhancing and rewarding that relationship.

When we worked with the Mirror Group, we set up a scheme with five thousand independent newsagents and the newsagents themselves became the communication channel to the consumer.

Within the business we use an enormous number of different ways to communicate with people, and one of the things that is creative about our business is looking at the best way to get a message in front of the right group of people.

When you do advertising, do you work in conjunction with ad agencies or do you do that in house?

We get another company to buy media on our behalf, but in terms of defining the brand, creating a strategy and developing creative concepts, we do that in house.

Where we differ from most other agencies is in our philosophy. We don't have a huge hierarchy, but a very flat structure. For example, we've formed a rolling body of agency personnel that are empowered to incite, implement and increase the rate of change within the agency. Everybody from the board to the most junior member of staff can take part.

A flatter hierarchy means we're more visible, too. At a lot of agencies the chief executive will walk in on day one and then disappear. The client never sees that person again and is left dealing only with a junior executive. That never happens at Mediator.

It's allowed us to build long-term relationships. We have been working with the Carphone Warehouse for five years. When we first started working with them they had forty-three shops. Now they are a pan-European business and have in excess of a thousand shops.

Other than the obvious one of the amount of money that you have at your disposal to do the advertising and so on, is there any difference in the strategy you will pursue when you're serving a smaller client?

No, there is no difference because we are media-neutral and don't have a preconceived idea about how to proceed.

As rule of thumb, what kind of financial commitment should a company be willing to make before bringing in an agency like yours to handle marketing?

By and large, our clients are public companies, like the BBC, British Airways, Choice Hotels, Sky Digital and the Carphone Warehouse, as I mentioned earlier. As an agency, I suppose we wouldn't look at a client who was going to spend anything less than a hundred thousand pounds in a year period. That said, if someone with less than that approaches us and we think the product or service has a lot of potential, then we will look at it.

We said to this client that I mentioned, 'We could sit here and say to you we are going to spend a half a million pounds for you.' But actually what we said to them was, 'Let's spend sixty thousand pounds researching, putting everything together and getting the communications strategy for marketing the product absolutely right. Then, if that comes out as being positive, the money you will spend going forward will be worthwhile.'

As part of the research report you give them, is there any estimate as to the kind of payoff they are likely to get for the money they're investing in the marketing?

Yes, we would look at it in terms of how much money they would spend and what the payback would be for every pound that they spend.

In your observation of what other companies have done, are there common errors in marketing?

One of the biggest errors was Internet companies spending huge sums on marketing without a real strategy. If you look at the Internet in its purest sense, it's one to one. On an Internet site you can talk to your consumers: you have that one-to-one exchange. So why spend huge amounts of money on advertising as a recruitment mechanism?

To use a frequently cited example, boo.com spent millions of pounds on promoting an Internet site that wasn't actually up and running and functional; that's like advertising a retail outlet in Oxford Street that isn't open yet.

What we have been doing with our dotcom clients is making sure that we target the right consumer group, and looking at the cost of the acquisition of customers. Everything should be quantifiable. Marketing gets a bad name when people don't use it to its full scientific extent. You can do things very scientifically; you can measure results.

So that might be one of the Ten Commandments of marketing. Are there other basics you feel are very important?

The most important thing is to make sure that you have a very clear brief. Are you trying to acquire customers? Are you trying to keep customers within your retail network? By questioning the brief at the very beginning and making sure that you as an agency and the client have the same perspective you end up having a much better relationship and much better results.

Some of the readers of this book are not going to be at the point where they are ready to work with an agency yet. Do you have any advice for them for DIY marketing, especially for individual operators or small businesses?

However small the business is, you should have some type of brand plan. You should look at where you are at the moment, where you want to be in six months, in a year, in three years, and the amount of money you are going to spend getting there.

What we do here is not complicated. It's about communication of a brand to the consumer. That requires that you know who your customers are: what kind of magazines they read, where they go on holiday, what kind of credit cards they have, where they go shopping at the weekend. The more you know about them, the easier it will be to come up with ways to get your message to them effectively. It doesn't necessarily require a massive amount of money.

Are there any brands you particularly admire in terms of their marketing, and, if so, what do you think has been the secret of their success?

I think that the great one to quote is Virgin. As a company, Virgin has a number of brands that stand in the consumers' eyes as being a consumers' champion. They do get a lot of criticism for having too many different products and for the problems with their train service, but by and large they have kept a great reputation in the eyes of the consumer, and that's a major accomplishment and has led to success in four or five different market sectors.

EasyJet is doing a similar kind of thing with rental cars, flights and Internet cafés. They have synergy across all their products. They are doing a great job with the consumer.

Our theme in this book is what people have done differently in order to be successful. You've touched on a few things Mediator does differently, but are there any others?

We recruit the top five per cent of people in this field. Most companies interview only when they are looking for someone to fill a particular position; we interview all the year round because that's the only way we can pick out the best people. Even if we haven't got something specifically that we think is a job opportunity, if somebody is very good we will take them on because we know we can find them a role in the company.

We also continually train our people. Every month we have a guest speaker from the industry. Last month we had one of the principals of New Media Investors, an incubator fund for dotcoms, because the best way for people to hear what's going on in dotcomland is not only to read what's going on but to speak to someone who is responsible for what gets funded.

We send people away on courses, we buy lots of equipment and books, and are continually making sure people continue to educate themselves.

At the very heart of the Mediator brand are the people that work here. Our vision is 'To Motivate People'. We want to create an environment where our staff is empowered, where they have the space to be as creative as they can be. But always with the goal of producing outstanding communications solutions that motivate our clients' customers. At the end of the day, we never forget it's a people thing.

Thank you. If people want to get in touch with Mediator, how can they do that?

They can ring 020 7436 3380, or they can go to the website, www.Mediator.co.uk.

Of course, it's ideal to have a team of experts such as those at Mediator or LCM working on your behalf, but perhaps your budget does not allow that yet. You can put together an effective marketing plan yourself by applying the key principles in this book, and the strategies that Lizz Clarke and Craig Newman describe. How to do that is covered in the next chapter.

How to Create Your Own Marketing Plan

In their interviews in the previous chapter, both Craig Newman and Lizz Clarke stressed that marketing is not some arcane black art: it's really about using common sense mixed with a dash of creativity. If you invest some time and effort in completing the following nine steps, you will have a plan that will guide you through the successful marketing of your product or service.

Step One

Define your target customer

As both Craig and Lizz say, if you try to reach everybody, your resources will be stretched so thin that you are unlikely to reach anybody.

I went through this with my newsletter. I believed (and still do) that everybody can benefit from being more creative, but I realised that it made sense to make my first target entrepreneurs who have small to medium-sized businesses.

Remember, you can always expand to include other groups when you have greater resources. My dream is that someday there will also be a *Brainstorm Junior* – a creativity newsletter that helps kids to hang on to their creativity as they grow up – but that will have to come at a later date. By all means, hang on to your dreams as well, but, for now, write down a concise definition of who you are trying to reach with your product or service.

Note all of the relevant characteristics of your target group: this could include their age range, the kind of work they do, their gender, their geographical location, their interests and their spending power, among others.

Step Two

Define what you are offering

Now that you know exactly who you are targeting, what are you offering them? What will your product or service do for them?

Be as complete in this description as possible. For example, if you are opening a restaurant, not only will you supply your customers with good food, but perhaps you will also offer them a romantic environment and a memorable experience. This is the message that you will be trying to convey to your target group as effectively as possible.

I hope in this description there will be what Tom Peters calls the 'wow! factor'. Don't be afraid to use poetic language in your description. Let us say that our restaurant will serve food that will delight even the most jaded palate, in an atmosphere that will turn even the coldest heart to warm thoughts of love, and with our caring service the evening will be one that our customers will talk about and relive in their imaginations for years to come! Well, if we're not aiming for that, what are we doing in the restaurant business?

Anyone reading your description should get excited, they should be desperate to buy this product or service. In today's world, mere competence is no longer enough, we all have to find a way not only to satisfy our customers, but also to delight them. If that element is missing from your product or service, you're not ready to market it yet, you need to go back to the drawing board until that wow! factor is present.

Condense your description into one simple sentence or phrase. What is the simple, powerful message that will tell people what is the essence of your product or service? For inspiration, notice the advertising slogans you hear every day: 'It's good to talk', or 'The world's favourite airline'. Pay attention to which messages really have an emotional impact on you and then try to give your message that same quality. In the case of our restaurant, we might decide that what we are promising our diners is 'a night to remember'.

Step Three

Define your goals

Now take a good look at where you are now with your business. Maybe you are just starting out, or maybe your business is established and ticking along but you'd like it to be more successful, or maybe it's already very successful but you'd like to take over the number-one slot in your field. Regardless, now jot down the relevant facts and figures. How many customers do you have? How many widgets do you sell? What is your annual gross? What are your annual expenses? What's your financial situation as regards debts and assets? And so on.

Also write down what position you hold relative to your competitors. You may not know exactly where you fit in, but you probably have a reasonable idea of how you measure up, both financially and in terms of your reputation.

With this in mind, decide where you'd like to be in five years, in three years, in two years, in one year and in six months. What kind of measure you use will depend upon your business and your perspective. You could define these goals in terms of your market share, your net income, your reputation in your field – most likely it will be a combination of measures. Start with the furthest one, five years, and work backward.

A useful digression about BHAGs

A word about goals. Most people don't think big enough when they set goals for themselves. Yes, there is the danger of being grandiose, but a greater danger, especially in the UK, is thinking too small. I would like to suggest that you set BHAGs (pronounced

Bee-Hags). In their excellent book *Built to Last*, James Collins and Jerry Porras state that having BHAGs (big, hairy, audacious goals) is one of the most important elements of enduring success. Here are the characteristics of BHAGs and how they work:

- BHAGs must be clear and compelling. That is, there must be a clear target, so that everyone will know when it is reached. And it has to be energising and highly focused, so it requires little or no explanation. For instance, Henry Ford set the goal of democratising the automobile – putting it within reach of the working man and woman.

- BHAGs must take people outside their normal comfort zone. They will thrive on the feeling that theirs is a heroic effort. Only then will they inspire a high degree of commitment. Queen Victoria once said, 'We are not interested in the possibility of defeat.' And neither are those who commit to BHAGs. Often it does not even occur to them that they might fail. As the authors point out, 'To set Big Hairy Audacious Goals requires a certain level of unreasonable confidence.' When John Kennedy made a commitment that the United States would put a man on the moon before the end of the decade, he was setting a risky BHAG.

- Corporate BHAGs must be bold and exciting enough to take on a life of their own, rather than being dependent on the enthusiasm of the leader. For example, Walt Disney's vision continues to inspire his company many years after his death.

- BHAGs must be consistent with the core values of the individual or company setting them. For the Merk Corporation, the core value is preserving and improving human life, and this value has infused their successful efforts to become one of the foremost drug makers in the world.

- BHAGs must be replaced with new BHAGs as soon as they are attained (or possibly a bit before they are attained), otherwise individuals and companies can become complacent and lose their momentum.

So … what is your BHAG? Is it big and audacious enough to inspire you when times are tough? Is it hairy enough to give you a thrill just thinking about it? Define your own BHAG, and then break it down into smaller components. It can be useful to give your goals a visual representation as well (a photo or illustration, for example), because our subconscious minds respond better to images than to words.

Step Four

Brainstorm all the ways you could convey your message to your target customers

If you use the questions and tips in this book as inspiration, you will be able to come up with dozens, maybe even hundreds, of ways of getting the attention of your potential customers. Brainstorm until you have a truly impressive and long list.

Don't judge them as you go along: wait until you have come up with lots and lots. One of my university professors was Linus Pauling, a Nobel Prize winner in the sciences. One day another student asked him to reveal the secret of his success, and he agreed to do so. 'The secret,' he said, 'is that I have lots and lots of ideas … and then I throw away the bad ones.' As a cosmic secret, this was a bit disappointing, but we realised that it held a serious message: let your mind wander freely, and only after you've come up with lots of ideas should you start to judge them, otherwise you will stifle your creativity.

Step Five

Find the ideas that fit the best (for now)

Now you have a clear picture of who you are trying to reach, the message you are trying to get to them and the resources you have at hand. With these in mind, go through your list of possible marketing approaches and start picking out the ones that seem to be most appropriate for now.

Some will be too expensive for you to do at the moment; some will require other resources you don't have yet; some may be too crazy to fit the product or service. Put those to one side, but don't throw them away, because they may be possible at another point in your marketing journey.

Step Six

Formulate your strategy

When you've winnowed down to the ideas that seem to fit best for achieving the six-month goal you have set for yourself, put them together into a strategy. Which does it make sense to do first? Which ones will logically lead to other ones? Again, remember what the pros said: this isn't voodoo, it's common sense and doing something different. Also remember that it does not have to be perfect, because you will adjust this plan as you go along.

When you have finished this step, you should have a map for the first six months. It can be very useful to get a large piece of paper and map out all the steps, with the six-month goal at the end. For each step, indicate the resources you will need (money, time, supplies, human beings) and where you are going to get them. Also, indicate exactly what you expect to gain from taking that step.

Step Seven

Take action and be patient

If you are a perfectionist, you may be tempted to spend too long on Step Six. Don't get hung up on designing the perfect plan, because it doesn't exist. Work hard to come up with a good plan, start implementing it, and, when it doesn't work the way you hoped, be ready to adjust it. But, as Lizz Clarke warned, be prepared for the fact that making an impact on the marketplace takes time.

By all means, learn from mistakes, tweak the plan as you go along, but stay with it.

Step Eight

Pay attention!

This isn't really a separate step: what I'm saying here is that you must not be so focused on your plan that you fail to notice other opportunities that come up as you go along. You will meet people and encounter opportunities that you didn't anticipate, and you must be flexible enough to take advantage of them quickly when they come up. When they do, always ask yourself whether they are consistent with reaching your BHAG and with your values and with your resources. If they are, go for it!

Equally, pay attention to what's working and not working. As Craig Newman said, marketing is measurable. Keep track of what works and what works even better. Take the chance to compare different methods whenever you can. For example, if you are going to run an ad in two magazines with similar readerships, try one headline in one ad and another in the other ad, and measure which gets the bigger response. If the ad has a coupon the reader sends in, make sure you code the coupons so you know which orders came from which ad.

Naturally your product or service does not operate in a vacuum, so also pay attention to what is happening in the world and the possible effects on your business in both the short and long term. The fluctuation in oil prices, for example, might have a short-term impact, and the fact that the population is skewing towards older people may have a long-term impact. When we are busy with our day-to-day functions, it's easy to forget to take a step back from time to time to look at the larger picture.

Step Nine

Do it all over again

The process I'm describing is ongoing. You should take time every three months or so to review your goals, review the impact of your marketing, review any changes you perceive in the target population, and so on.

And please don't forget: enjoy it!

Yes, we want to make a good living – maybe we even want to be filthy rich – but let's not forget to enjoy ourselves along the way and keep a balance between our business life and our personal life. Having worked in Hollywood for a number of years, I've met quite a few filthy-rich and very miserable people. Why miserable? Because their last film didn't make as much money as the one before that, or as much money as their chief rival's, or because their swimming pool is a foot shorter than the neighbour's. I'm not exactly sure why you and I are on this earth, but worrying about that sort of thing probably isn't it!

Fortunately, most of the 'do something different' strategies in this book are playful and fun, and it's almost guaranteed that you'll enjoy yourself in your journey to success. It's always good to have a full set of resources available, and in the next chapter I recommend some that I think will help you along the way.

Resources For Your Journey

 Books

There has been an explosion of titles about marketing in the last few years. Here are some of the best:

Re-imagine! Business Excellence in a Disruptive Age, Tom Peters (Dorling Kindersley, 2004). Peters is part business guru, part cheerleader, and a great read if you ever find your energy flagging. Half the time he's on target, half the time he's over the top; it's never easy to tell which half is which – and that's part of the fun of reading him.

What Makes Winning Brands Different, Wolfram Woerdermann and Andreas Buchholz (John Wiley & Sons, Ltd, 2000). This book takes a close look at the variety of emotional appeals that can make consumers fall in love with a brand.

The Experience Economy, B Joseph Pine II and James H Gilmore (Harvard Business School Press, 1999). Pine and Gilmore maintain that these days work is theatre and every business is a stage. They give a good insight into how you can turn the process of buying into an enjoyable experience for the customer.

Guerrilla Marketing Attack, Jay Conrad Levinson (Houghton Mifflin Co., 1989). Levinson has become the guru of guerrilla marketing and this book, as well as his original *Guerrilla Marketing*, is full of useful strategies and tips.

The New Marketing Manifesto, John Grant (Texere, 1999). A convincing look at how some of the basic notions of marketing have been changing, with a number of interesting case studies, including Tango, Egg and the Spice Girls.

The books of **Mark McCormack** are also worth your time. His first was *What They Don't Teach You at Harvard Business School*, published in 1988. Since then he's walked his talk and become a multimillionaire. His latest is *Staying Street Smart in the Internet Age* (2000), and he has also written one of the best of the obnoxiously named 'Dummy' books: *Getting Results for Dummies* (2000).

A no-nonsense, very entertaining writer is **Dan Kennedy**, whose books include *How To Make a Million From Your Ideas* (1996) and *No Rules* (with Scott DeGarmo, 1998). Kennedy has made most of his money by telling others how to make money, but the information he imparts is no less valid for that.

Magazines

Among the magazines that regularly offer excellent articles on marketing are *Fast Company*, *Business 2.0*, *Wired*, *Forbes*, *Inc.*, *Success*, *Entrepreneur*, and *Red Herring*.

For insights into consumer behaviour, keep an eye on *Psychology Today*.

For articles on creativity, naturally I recommend my own monthly *Brainstorm* email bulletin. I will be happy to send you the email bulletin free every month if you send your details to BstormUK@aol.com or the address at the end of this chapter.

I also recommend that every month you pick up at least a couple of magazines that are totally outside your field of business, and even outside your field of interest, just so you can see what's going on. You may find marketing ideas that you can adapt to your field.

The Internet

For starters, each of the magazines listed above has a website. However, as you know, things change very quickly on the Internet, so, rather than list websites that may be gone by the time you see this, I suggest that you access my site, www.BrainstormNet.com, and click on the 'Do Something Different' page. There you will find links to the dozen best marketing sites available at the time, plus reviews of the best of the new books on marketing, plus an archive of additional case histories like the ones you've found in this book.

Why not be a resource yourself?

If you come up with your own innovative approach to marketing and are willing to share your success story, we'd love to put it on the website and possibly in the next edition of this book. As the world is becoming aware, when we share our knowledge, we gain rather than lose. Please also send any comments or suggestions you might have regarding this book. I would be delighted to hear from you.

> Jurgen Wolff
> Brainstorm
> 85 Ridgmount Gardens
> London WC1E 7AY
> United Kingdom
> Email: J4London@AOL.com
> Website: www.BrainstormNet.com

Index

CENTRE FOR SMALL & MEDIUM SIZED ENTERPRISES

Warwick is one of a handful of European business schools that have won a truly global reputation. Its high standards of both teaching and research are regularly confirmed by independent ratings and assessments.

The Centre for Small & Medium Sized Enterprises (CSME) is one of the school's major research centres. We have been working with people starting a business, or already running one, since 1985. The Centre also helps established companies to reignite the entrepreneurial flame that is essential for any modern business.

We don't tell entrepreneurs what to do – just help them be more aware and better informed of the opportunities and pitfalls of running a growing small enterprise.

Much of our practical knowledge is gleaned from the experience of individuals who themselves have been there and done it. These kinds of business coaches rarely commit their observations to paper, but in this Virgin/Warwick series they have captured in print their passion and their knowledge. It's a new kind of business publishing that addresses the constantly evolving challenge of business today.

For more information about Warwick Business School (courses, owner networks and other support to entrepreneurs, managers and new enterprises), please contact:

Centre for Small & Medium Sized Enterprises
Warwick Business School
University of Warwick
Coventry CV4 7AL
UK
Tel: +44 (0) 2476 523741 (CSME); or 524306 (WBS)
Fax: +44 (0) 2476 523747 (CSME); or 523719 (WBS)
Email: enquiries@wbs.warwick.ac.uk
And visit CSME's partner website, the Mercia Institute of Enterprise, via: www.merciainstitute.com
Tel: +44 (0) 2476 574002

Also available in the Virgin Business Guides series:

CUSTOMER IS KING
HOW TO EXCEED THEIR EXPECTATIONS
Robert Craven

ISBN 0 7535 0968 7

KICK-START YOUR BUSINESS
100 DAYS TO A LEANER, FITTER ORGANISATION
Robert Craven

ISBN 0 7535 0973 3

THE BEST-LAID BUSINESS PLANS
HOW TO WRITE THEM, HOW TO PITCH THEM
Paul Barrow

ISBN 0 7535 0963 6

THE BOTTOM LINE
BUSINESS FINANCE: YOUR QUESTIONS ANSWERED
Paul Barrow

ISBN 0 7535 0998 9

PR POWER
INSIDE SECRETS FROM THE WORLD OF SPIN
Amanda Barry

ISBN 0 7535 0904 0

DOING THE BUSINESS
BOOST YOUR COMPANY'S FORTUNES
David Hall

ISBN 0 7535 0680 7

IT'S NOT ABOUT SIZE
BIGGER BRANDS FOR SMALLER BUSINESSES
Paul Dickinson

ISBN 0 7535 0593 2

20/20 HINDSIGHT
FROM STARTING UP TO SUCCESSFUL
ENTREPRENEUR, BY THOSE WHO'VE BEEN THERE
Rachelle Thackray

ISBN 0 7535 0547 9

LITTLE e, BIG COMMERCE
HOW TO MAKE A PROFIT ONLINE
Timothy Cumming

ISBN 0 7535 0542 8